Clear
Channel

Clear
Channel

A Guide for the
Newly Awakening

Wendy Joy
Reiki Master Teacher

BALBOA.
PRESS
A DIVISION OF HAY HOUSE

Balboa Press books may be ordered through booksellers or by contacting:

Balboa Press
A Division of Hay House
1663 Liberty Drive
Bloomington, IN 47403
www.balboapress.com
1-(877) 407-4847

ISBN: 978-1-4525-3332-2 (sc)
ISBN: 978-1-4525-3334-6 (hc)
ISBN: 978-1-4525-3333-9 (e)

Library of Congress Control Number: 2011903947

Printed in the United States of America

Balboa Press rev. date: 8/22/2011

In Loving Memory of Karen—
You lived your life well.
You touched so many lives in ways you never understood.
You showed me what friendship is.
Thank you for your love.

I love you, too.

Wendy

To
Mary, Joanna & James
You have my eternal love.

To
The Others –
Remember who you are.
We welcome you when you are ready.

Be Well,
Rebekah

A Book of Remembering

Disclaimer

I stand behind the content of this book in the sense that it is absolutely true for me at this point in time. I reserve the right to modify it as I am presented with new guidance. Occasionally, I am presented with an updated or expanded truth after I've incorporated the one given previously. I would ask that you evaluate the ideas presented against your own guidance as well, and that you seek professional guidance when making medical/healing decisions. Never give your power away by blindly accepting what others say. That includes me.

Acknowledgments

Writing this book was one of the most humbling yet exciting events of my life. I am fully aware that I did not write it on my own. I had tremendous assistance from the spiritual and physical worlds. For this blessing, I am eternally grateful.

Foremost, I'd like to thank Frank, my partner in this life, for your continual support. We've known each other for most of this lifetime and you have always allowed me to be who I am—even when that shifted completely.

Julie, I don't know the words to thank you for how you've transformed my life. I believe that being around your energy is what triggered my awakening. What bigger gift is there than that?

Andrea, how far we've come together. What a beautiful plan it was to learn from each other as we went through this awakening. I can't wait to see where God leads us from here.

Tracy, how fortunate I am to have you in my life. Your many questions helped me clarify my thinking so I could learn the lessons more fully. I love that you always thought I'd know the answers!

Karen, I miss you deeply. You taught me true friendship. I've never seen anyone care for friends like you did. Your life was hard and much too short, but you taught us many lessons. You experienced pain, but you also grasped onto and acknowledged the joy in life like no one I've ever seen. Please keep watching over me, Frank, and "your red-headed kids."

Eric and Molly, my son and daughter, you are my inspirations. I love it that energy and Angels are such a natural part of your world. You've taught me more in these few short years than you'll ever know.

To my mom and dad, Henrietta and Ronald Schofield; my mother-in-law, Betty Ellmo; and my aunt, Dorothy Wood, thank you for your love, generosity and support. I appreciate how you always jumped in to help us hold things together logistically. Thanks also for going through this shift without judgment. Poppy, I miss you.

Will Linville, you provided so much guidance, clarity and healing when it was so needed. Your love of life and all people is an example for the world. When I was frustrated, it gave me strength just knowing you were there with answers that would change my perspective.

Thank you, Joy Gardner, for your masterful editing. Your wonderful command of the language and your knowledge of the content made you the perfect choice.

To my many clients and friends, I give thanks. You taught me so many things that you will see in these pages.

Spirit—all the Angels, guides, Avatars, elementals and others who came to help me—thank you. This book became what it is supposed to be because of you.

May this book be and do all that God intended.

Contents

Acknowledgments xi

Foreword by Joy Gardner xvii

Introduction xix

    Evolution and Awakening xxiii

    Reluctant Writer xxv

    Call Back in the Morning xxvi

    Religion xxvii

    Public Revelation xxix

    Further Confirmation xxix

    Becoming a Reiki Master Teacher xxx

    Operator's Guide xxxi

1   Energy: Can You Feel It? 1

    How to Feel Energy 2

    Vibrations in the Night 4

    Head Rocking 5

    Chakra Clearings 7

    Seeing Colors 8

    More Vibrations 9

    Collective Consciousness 10

    Becoming Empathic 11

2   Building to Conscious Contact: Intuition and Beyond 15

    Concrete Signs 15

    Body-Level Intuition 21

    Higher Level Intuition 24

    Conscious Contact 28

    Need-to-Know Basis 29

    Developing a Clear Connection 30

    Let Go of the Ego 32

    Growing in Guidance 33

3   Allowing and Prayer: Be Open 35

    Be Still 35

    Watch Your Thoughts 37

    "Lord, Bless this Garbage" 39

    Help Yourself 40

Deadly Beliefs 42

We Need All the Help We Can Get! 43

Do Your Part 44

There Are No Accidents 45

4   Speak the Truth: What's Your Truth? 47

Out of My Comfort Zone 48

Mistaken Motives 49

Follow the Nudge 50

Share Your Truth 52

Don't Worry About Others' Opinions 52

Speak for the Benefit of Others 54

The Truth is Not Absolute 54

5   Awakenings: Everybody Up! 57

Good Vibrations 58

Nighttime Healings 58

Nighttime Travel 59

Give Me Strength 60

Numbers in the Night 60

Messages in the Night 61

Embrace the Night 63

6   Operate From Love: Are You Feeling the Love? 65

Seven Tools to Increase Your Ability to Operate from Love: 66

Our Biggest Challenges 70

7   Fluctuations: Here We Go Again 73

Bad Times 74

Choices 75

Get It Yourself 76

The Reason We Go Slowly 77

Wind-Up Airplanes 78

Fluctuations in Accuracy 80

Stupid Plan 81

8   Healing: You Are Perfect and Whole 83

Continue to Watch Your Thoughts 83

Identify the Message 84

Health Challenges as Lessons 86

Examples of Healing 88

Breaking Patterns 90

You Are Never Alone 91

The Importance of Human Form 91

You Can Help Others to Heal 93

Distant Healing 95

Keys for Healing 97

9   Be Well: Additional Healing Concepts 101
     Onions 101
     Let it ALL Go 103
     Healing "Past" Lives 103
     Leave it in the "Past" 104
     Perfect at Birth 105
     How Fast Do You Want to Go? 106
     Decisions and Exit Points 107
     Astral Travel 108
     Transitional Opportunities 109
     Additional Keys for Healing 110

10 Know Your Power: You Are Powerful 111
     We Are Powerful 112
     Break from the Collective Consciousness 114
     Manifesting What You Desire 115
     Back to Manifesting 116
     Growing in Power 117
     Warping Time 118
     Time to Heal 118
     Miracles and Mother Earth 119
     Sharing Abilities across Lifetimes 120
     Helping to Pass 121
     Higher Self to Higher Self 122
     Don't Give Your Power Away 123
     Humility 124
     Multidimensional Beings 125
     This and More 126

11 Divine Life Purpose: Live Your Joy 127
     Drop Your Ego 128
     Explore Your Gifts 129
     Live YOUR Life 130
     The Flip Side 132
     Catch the Ball 132
     Simple Plans 133
     Show Me 134
     Follow Your Purpose 135
     Pre-incarnation Checklist 136
     Purpose Plus Joy Equals Success 136

12 Clearing Energy: Getting Unstuck! 139
     Symptoms 140
     Techniques for Clearing 141
     Clearing Another Person's Energy from Your Own 143
     Breaking Energetic Ties ("Cords") 145

13 Support From Others: Don't Go It Alone 147
    Spiritual Family 147
    Crazy Together 149
    Total Trust 150
    Finding Like-Minded Friends 151
    Complementary Messages 151
    This One's for You 153
    Support Each Other 153
    Share with Your Mate 154
    Teach the Children Well 155
    The Religions 156
    Calling All Angels 157
    Asking for Help and Support 157

14 Jesus: A Loving Role Model 159
    The Reminder 160
    Jesus Visits 162
    Confirmation 163
    Where Are We Going? 164
    A Simple Life 165
    What If? 167
    Sin vs. Karma 168
    Why Not Buddha? 169

15 Ghosts: Who's There? 171
    The Sitting Room 172
    Find a Better Light 173
    Turn Off the Light 174
    Careful Whom You Call 175

Conclusion: Or Is It Just The Beginning? 177

Notes 181

About the Author 185

Foreword

By Joy Gardner

I wish I had a book like this back in the sixties, when I was experiencing my own spiritual awakening. I felt like a stranger in a strange land. There were no guideposts, and I vacillated between feeling like some sort of saint and feeling like a madwoman. I questioned every impulse; I second-guessed my guidance; and I doubted the insights that came unbidden.

This is the perfect guidebook to help beginners navigate the fierce, tumultuous and glorious waters of their own soul journeys. Even more than that, this book provides alternative healing practitioners—and their students—with an overwhelming sense of *certainty* that this work is real, valid, and *powerful*! Even if you're experienced at holistic healing, it's hard to avoid what Wendy calls the Collective Consciousness, which tells us that the work we are doing is simply not possible!

Thank you, Wendy, for strengthening my own belief in myself, and allowing me to feel even more confident about the incredible work I am doing! You've strengthened my faith in myself, in my Angels, and in God, and you've done so in a truly entertaining way. What more could a book possibly do?

—Joy Gardner, author of eleven books, including *Vibrational Healing through the Chakras with Light, Color, Sound, Crystals and Aromatherapy* and Director of the Vibrational Healing Certification Program.

Introduction

I'm a Speech Language Pathologist, a wife, and the mother of two teenage children. When this story began, I was working for a prestigious brain trauma facility on the East Coast. My spiritual awakening started when I saw a "For Sale by Owner" sign on a house on the coast of North Carolina. I began to see things, feel things, and know things that I never knew before.

But I'm getting ahead of myself . . . .

I was raised as a Protestant. I was a good girl. I went to church regularly and I enjoyed it. Church was a social place for me; not a spiritual one. I learned to have good morals and do unto others as I would have them do unto me. I didn't get a sense of spirituality or God or Angels. I never felt heavenly support.

Nothing occurred that sent me looking for more information or hope of a Higher Power. I grew up thinking that the familiar Biblical quotes, like, "The truth shall set you free," or "Ask and it is given," were good guidelines to follow so we could all get along.

I was an athlete and scholar in high school. I worked hard and tried to do the right thing.

When I was seventeen, I was riding in a car with some friends when the car was broadsided as we crossed a highway at a faulty traffic light. I was thrown out of the backseat, flipped in the air and I landed on the back of my head in the middle of an intersection. I guess I blacked out for a while because my next memory was of awakening moments later with a knowing in my head: "Get up. It's not safe here." I stumbled up to a curb and sat down, looking at the pretty red drops dripping onto my knee.

I was taken to the hospital in an ambulance, treated and released. I had a concussion and the bones in my neck were badly misaligned. I immediately went back to school, to my part-time job at a pizzeria and my life as usual—except that I was in continuous pain. I had a headache that lasted two years, and neck and back pain that lasted twenty-two years.

Frank had been in a car behind us. He started coming by my parents' house to check on me. He was nineteen. I could talk to him about anything. We talked a lot about existentialism and the meaning of life. It bothered me that I almost died and yet I saw no purpose in life or death. I couldn't account for the minutes I was unconscious. There was just nothing; not even darkness. Nothing. I reasoned that that was what death was.

My chronic pain led to anger at God. How could He do this to me?

Frank became my best friend. A few months later, without even kissing him, I realized I was in love.

Frank had a firm Catholic faith, but he didn't really share it with me, probably because he knew I couldn't hear it at that point.

Mom soon became aware that I was forgetting things. She had to drop off a lot of forgotten lunches and assignments at school. Andrea, my good friend since grade school, realized, too. I didn't notice.

My college search began and I found the perfect school in North Carolina—five hundred miles away from my home in New Jersey. I always dreamed of going away to college, and Frank understood. That September I left for Duke University. I felt like my heart was being ripped from my chest.

At Duke, I had difficulty with attention and concentration. It took me much longer to do assignments that would have been quick for me in the past. I couldn't focus my attention, and my memory was bad. I was pulling off good grades, but the effort was crippling. I didn't relate it to the car accident because the doctors told me I was fine.

During my first summer break, my mother heard a public service announcement sponsored by the Brain Injury Association of America about post concussive syndrome and she thought it sounded like me. She found a brain injury program nearby and they scheduled me for Speech Therapy and Counseling. I wouldn't talk to the Counselor about anything bothering me. I was raised as a stoic English/German and we didn't do that! Instead, I reserved my feelings for Frank. We had progressed to a romantic relationship and we took every opportunity we could find in our class schedules to visit each other.

The Speech Language Pathologist was phenomenal. As the title implies, they work on speech (the motor aspects of speaking) and language (how we put our ideas together to communicate them), but they also work on cognition—thinking. This was her focus with me. I was fascinated as she taught me strategies to compensate for my attention and concentration. But I was also mad, because I didn't want to compensate; I wanted it to be fixed. But I was amazed by all that went into the process of thinking and how to improve it when it went wrong. I was also fascinated by the patients with brain injuries that I met there; they were all so unique and brave.

I returned to Duke for my sophomore year, with a new determination to become a Speech Language Pathologist specializing in brain injury. My undergraduate years were still hard, but now I had a strategy for each new situation. I graduated in three years so I could hurry up and go to graduate school, get back to New Jersey and be with Frank—and to prove to myself that I was still smart.

During this time, as life got better, my anger at God eased. I never believed in a punitive God and I didn't think there was anything I needed to be punished for, so the accident must have been a random occurrence. I wasn't even sure I believed in God. I began to think I might be an atheist.

Following graduation, I married Frank and went to work for the same brain trauma facility that had treated me.

My life goal was to work hard and do well. Since there was no *real* purpose to life, I would just achieve as much as I could and live a good life. I treated my clients well and tried to be the best Speech Language Pathologist I could be. I became President of our state Speech Language Pathology association and worked on many state and national committees. I published a book of treatment activities, some papers, and a test for language disorders following brain injury. I was always busy. To me, that was success, and I was happy.

I was trying to fit yoga into my schedule, to curtail my pain and keep some semblance of the fitness I enjoyed in my younger years. That's where I met Julie, with her jet-black hair pulled back into a ponytail and just a hint of an accent revealing her Spanish heritage. She was an oncology nurse at a specialized cancer center. She was clearly on a spiritual path (she majored in Comparative Religion) and I could talk to her about almost anything. We became close friends.

Then Andrea, my friend from high school, moved to a nearby town. We readily reconnected as we relived our high school days and bonded over the joys and stresses of being working moms. It was easy to convince Andrea to join Julie and me for the yoga classes. Andrea and Julie hit it off from the start. I found that Julie's calm, measured responses served as a good balance to Andrea's quick wit and call-it-like-I-see-it attitude.

Many years passed. During the summers, Frank and I loved to take our two kids to vacation at the beach in North Carolina. Sometimes Andrea's and Julie's families would join us. We had a favorite island that I learned about from a dear friend who had been my college roommate. Carolyn had spent the summer on the island and raved about it. When Frank and I got married, Carolyn was our bridesmaid. Three months later, she was killed by a drunk driver. I missed her, and I noticed that I felt closer to her when I was on the island. I guess her parents did, too, because they moved there after her death.

On this trip, I saw the sign for that house for sale that I mentioned earlier. We weren't looking for a house, but I felt like I was being pulled there by my heart. I don't know how else to explain it. I called the owner. His name was Peter and he made it sound like it was a major inconvenience to show us the house. He had all kinds of things he needed to do. I persisted and finally he said, "Listen, if you can come right now, I'll show it to you." We went right away.

Peter rushed us through the house and out the garage. There was a pickup truck backed into the garage with a novelty Duke license plate in the back window. I didn't mention my connection to Duke because I didn't get the sense he'd want to talk. I walked around to the front of the truck and there was another Duke license plate. That was too much for me. So I said, "Do you have children that went to Duke?"

He looked at me as if for the first time and said, "You know, you may be about her age. Do you mind if I ask how old you are?"

I said, "Sure, I'm thirty-eight."

Then he said, "Did you know Carolyn Sonzogni?"

"She was my roommate."

We all had goosebumps. Peter said, "This is her father's truck. Had you not come right now, this truck would not have been here. It wasn't here yesterday and it won't be here tomorrow. I borrowed it to take some things to a flea market."

I knew then why I had been pulled to see that house. Carolyn was showing it to me. She liked to crack jokes, so maybe she was doing it just to have fun with me. But where did I get that idea? I didn't believe in life after death. And yet, this incident opened me up to the idea that there was more going on here than meets the eye. By the way, we never did buy that house.

That was November. The following spring, our favorite yoga instructor, Lindy, was learning a hands-on energy healing practice called Reiki. She was calling all her students, looking for volunteers to practice on. I was a likely target because of my chronic pain issues. It was a wonderfully calming experience. I didn't tell her where the pain was, and yet her hands stopped every place I had pain or an injury or a sensation of heat. I had broken both of my elbows rollerblading several years before, and her hands stopped at my elbows even though I no longer felt any pain there. Lindy had known me for several years, so I didn't think much of it. She *could* know where my pain was, I rationalized. I was taking the easy way out.

Following the session, I had a peace I never experienced before. I knew I had to become a Reiki practitioner.

Evolution and Awakening

After the Reiki session, I began having strange experiences, where I would know things, sense them and see them. The same thing was happening to Andrea. She and I were initially hesitant to share what was happening because it was so subtle, so hard to describe, so out of the ordinary, and I guess we each felt like maybe we were going crazy. Since Julie was familiar with so many different religions, we each began to share our experiences with her. That's when we learned that she was having similar revelations, but to a more extreme degree.

Thank God we shared. I began journaling about what was happening right from the start. I never showed up anywhere with those two ladies without a notebook and pen close by.

What Julie, Andrea and I began to experience was not unique to us. We, as a species, are evolving into what David R. Hawkins, M.D., Ph.D. calls *Homo spiritus*,[1] spiritual man. According to Hawkins, "The term 'Homo spiritus' refers to the awakened man who has bridged the evolutionary leap from physical to spiritual, from form to nonform, and from linear to nonlinear."[2] Homo spiritus marks a move from the thinking man of Homo sapiens, capable of reasoning and abstraction, to spiritual awareness and recognition of God as Creator and the force behind all things.

Eckhart Tolle, a spiritual teacher and author who is much loved by Oprah Winfrey, calls us a new species[3], "with a new consciousness.[4] According to Tolle, in *A New Earth: Awakening to Your Life's Purpose*, we are being forced beyond thinking to evolve to a new level of consciousness, to an awakening.[5] For Tolle, awakening is becoming aware that you exist beyond your thoughts. There is another self that is capable of looking at the thoughts. For some, the awakening is instantaneous; for others it occurs over time, through ongoing life experiences.

This change in spirituality is not just happening inside of religious establishments. In fact, the majority of it appears to be happening outside of these institutions, in the hearts of people all around the globe. Tolle writes, "We are witnessing . . . an unprecedented influx of consciousness at this time."[6]

A growing number of people are experiencing a knowing that they are here for a purpose, yet are frustrated because they have no idea what it is. Many people are feeling a buzzing or vibration in their bodies, especially in the quiet of the night.

"This doesn't apply to me," you might say. "I haven't experienced any of this."

Yet.

According to Hawkins, this evolution is directly related to a change in the energy of the Earth, which is causing a vibrational shift in man. This evolution brings with it a potential and a demand for change in all of us. We are now capable of feeling and manipulating energy within and around us; we have the potential to increase our intuition to levels we never dreamed possible. We have the opportunity to operate from a position of love that many of us have never experienced before.

This evolution brings with it challenges to discover our truth and to take on our divine life purpose—the reason we incarnated here at this time. We have the potential to experience many wondrous gifts, including healing, manifesting objects and situations, and working in full partnership with the spirit world. For many, it brings disruption of our once-normal everyday lives, including sleep patterns, emotions and relationships.

Perhaps this is happening to you—or to your friends or relatives. You may have dismissed these experiences as odd coincidences or flukes. You may have experienced knowing something was going to happen before it occurred—even something inconsequential, like knowing the phone was going to ring. You may have thought about someone you haven't seen in years—only to have that person email you later in the day, out of nowhere.

Maybe you have met someone for the first time, but felt like you knew each other for a lifetime. You may have placed your hand on an ache and felt heat, or relief from pain. Perhaps you wished for something to occur and then watched as circumstances miraculously transpired to make it happen. You may have noticed, while sitting in a class or meeting, bored, with your eyes slightly out of focus, that a pale outline appeared around the speaker's head and shoulders. You may have woken up with a feeling that you need to do something, but don't know what.

You are not imagining things. This is happening more often to more people, as the energy around us shifts and causes us to open to our true potential as spirit in human form.

Reading this book will likely open you up. Unusual experiences may begin to happen. Or you may begin to realize that they have been happening for a long time; you just haven't given them any weight. You dismissed them, or attributed them to something concrete, as many of us do. As I did.

Reluctant Writer

I didn't set out to write a book. I was just trying to live my life, day by day. Somehow this book found me. It began very simply and innocently. I began journaling as Julie and Andrea and I began to experience increases in our intuition and a sense of knowing that seemed to come from outside ourselves. We called it "guidance." We would each initially get parts of a message that we would piece together. We later learned that there were always multiple layers to most messages. We might have dismissed it as imagination if it hadn't been happening to all three of us. Julie has always received guidance from Spirit, even as a young girl, so she gave us a lot of support as we moved along.

I began the journal long before I realized there was a book. Slowly the knowing grew that there was a book, and William Linville confirmed it. I met Will through a speech client. Will is beyond what we normally think of as psychic. He has the clearest connection to Spirit and to his guides that I have ever known. I was blessed to meet him several years ago and have since visited him for guidance, clarity and healing a couple times a year. Upon meeting Will, I was struck by the love that he embodies and his true passion and excitement for life. Throughout the book, I refer to information that he provided, which helped to shed light on so many events in our lives.

I thought it comical that I was to write a book about spiritual things. I had written professionally in the areas that I had been trained in: speech language pathology and brain injury. But I was just a novice in the area of spirituality, energy, intuition and healing. But I remained open to the possibility because it triggered a knowing down deep, that writing this book was something I came here to do.

Over time, I began to understand that the journal would become a book. But this made no sense, because the journal contained random chronological events that were in no way linked or ordered. Or were they?

Early on in writing, I sensed that the book was a guide and that was confirmed as I went along. The "Clear Channel" part of the title was given to me by Spirit. As we evolve spiritually and heal physically, mentally and emotionally, we are clearing our channels: our physical bodies and energy fields, or auras, around us. This clearing allows us to evolve even further and to step into our full potential as spirit in human form.

Call Back in the Morning
My sense of needing to write began to build, even as my confusion about what to write increased. I began to see signs that it was time to get writing. For three nights, I kept waking up at exactly 2:39 am. I argued with Spirit, saying that I didn't need to get up and write because I could write during the day, in between my other duties, during normal waking hours. But Spirit had other ideas, and I continued to wake up at 2:39. The number appeared to be beckoning me. I looked it up in Doreen Virtue

and Lynnette Brown's book, *Angel Numbers: the angels explain the meaning of 111, 444 and other numbers in your life*, and it said, "The ascended masters say, 'Get to work on your life purpose now!' and ask you to have faith in your abilities to make a difference in the world. You and your mission are needed."[7]

The experience of being awakened in the night was not new to me. About three years prior, I was routinely wakened nightly to meditate. At first I didn't know why I kept waking, but a slow knowing began to grow. Now I knew that I'd continue to be awakened until I wrote. So, I wrote. After a few nights, the door to the adjoining sitting room blew open at 2:39, with a warm welcoming energy. Opening in the night was not something this door did. It stayed shut unless there was a significant wind. Of course, there had been no wind.

Over the next three months, the bulk of the book was written, almost exclusively in the middle of the night, as a co-creation with Spirit. I rarely knew exactly what I was to write, and I did not hear a clear voice speaking to me. Yet I felt a presence each time I was writing, and I could call on that presence for assistance when I needed a word, a phrase or a forgotten thought.

The names of many of the people in this book were changed to protect their privacy. Some of the circumstances have also been altered, but the messages and lessons have been preserved.

Religion

For me, talk of spiritual growth is independent of religion. Spirit is all around us, whether we are Protestants, Catholics, Jews, Muslims or atheists. I thought it was funny that God believed in me even when I didn't believe in Him. But my profound experiences with hands-on healing renewed my faith in God. I went back to church, and became part of an adult Sunday school program about learning to do what Jesus did. The pastor talked about a boy named Adam in Canada, who was healing people with his hands. The tone in the room turned to excitement. This is what we were here to learn, and the pastor was telling us about someone who was actually doing it. By this point, I had been doing Reiki for about two years, so I was comfortable with the concept. The energy in the room was building as he gave more examples of the boy's healings.

Then suddenly the pastor declared, "But he never said whose name he did it in."

The pastor's own wife said, "What do you mean? Whose name *could* he be doing it in?"

"Satan's name" was his response. I immediately deflated, as did the rest of the room. But I got up the courage to stand up and tell about my experience with Reiki (without using the term, because I knew from previous discussions that he had a problem with Reiki). I told everyone about how the energy began to flow through and around my hands and they felt like they were enveloped in warmth. When that happened, I exclaimed out loud, "Oh my God . . . You are there!"

It was in that moment that I knew, beyond any measure of doubt, that God exists. There was no question in my mind that it was from God. I told the pastor that I could understand why the boy wouldn't feel the need to say who was doing the actual healing, because perhaps for him, like me, it was too obvious to need stating.

The pastor wasn't buying it, and a pall remained on the room.

After that, I parted ways with formal religion. The pastor's caution did not fit my personal experience of healing as God-given, pure and loving, and I didn't feel comfortable worshipping in a place of fear. I respect the world's religions and the comfort and joy they provide for people. But I part company with religions once they attempt to take away my personal power by instilling fear or a sense of obligation.

Spirituality is independent of the words we use to describe it. I use the words "Spirit, God, and Angels" because I conceptualize things in this way because of my religious upbringing. Those who were raised as Buddhists, for example, will use different words to describe their spiritual experiences. But I believe that we are all talking about the same Divine Energy, the same all-pervasive love.

I use the word Spirit, with a capital S, when I haven't identified exactly who was present. Spirit for me means positive, non-physical entities, like the Avatars (enlightened teachers such as Jesus and Buddha) or the Angels. When I refer to the spirit of a person (passed or living), I use spirit with a small s.

I use the term ghosts (see Chapter 15) to describe non-Angelic, non-Avatar presences who have not crossed through the light and are currently stuck here. They feel very different from the higher vibration Spirits. I think I needed to experience their presence so that I could make people aware of them and how to assist them.

I am now aware of Jesus being with me as one of my guides, and I now have a very personal relationship with Jesus (see Chapter 14). I feel closer to this great Avatar than I ever did in church. I see Jesus as one of many Avatars. But my spiritual view extends beyond the views of any one religion. I consider myself a student of all religions and a seeker of the highest truth, wherever I might find it. I find great joy in discovering what I believe to be the underlying truths that unite all religions.

Public Revelation

Honestly, I'm not comfortable revealing so much about my personal life and my spiritual beliefs. I know there are many who will think I am crazy or even sinful. I have considered that possibility, too, though I discard it on *most* days! I was perfectly content to have my little experiences and live my little life with only *some* of my family and friends knowing what was happening. But Spirit was clear that the lessons being taught through my life were meant for a larger audience.

I worried about what people would say for a while, and that delayed my writing. Then I began to understand that sharing this information is one of my sacred contracts. It is one of the things I hoped I would do, if I ever made it to this point, in this incarnation. I desire to live on purpose. If that means sharing something that a family member, or a co-worker, or a friend, or someone *I never even met* thinks is crazy or sinful, then so be it. I will have done what I know is important for me, in this lifetime. I wish the same for you.

Further Confirmation

In 2007, I read Joy Gardner's book, *Vibrational Healing through the Chakras with Light, Color, Sound, Crystals and Aromatherapy*. I resonated with everything she wrote about. Months later, I was delighted to hear that she would be teaching in New York, just a few hours from where I lived. I signed up for her Vibrational Healing Certification Program—nine workshops on a variety of topics that were all in perfect alignment with what I had been experiencing. Within a year-and-a-half, I became a certified Vibrational Healer. But more important, I developed a new confidence in myself and in the experiences I was having. I felt validated.

By this time I was nearly done with the book, and I asked Joy if she would like to read the manuscript. I was delighted when she agreed, and even more pleased when she told me how much she enjoyed the book, and offered to edit it. I accepted, of course, and as she worked on the book, she liked it so much that she volunteered to write the Foreword. It felt like one more confirmation of the messages I had received from my own guidance and from Will. And it renewed my commitment to getting this book published!

Becoming a Reiki Master Teacher

By the time I met Joy Gardner, I was already a Reiki Master Teacher and I was an advanced Integrated Energy Practitioner. Becoming attuned to Reiki energy was one of the most significant positive experiences of my life. I sought out Reiki training initially to heal myself and that's basically all I used it for in the beginning. Once I saw the benefits of the energy in my life, I began to use it to help others, with amazing results. I share several of these stories in the following pages.

Through a Reiki attunement, a Reiki Master Teacher aligns you with the Reiki vibration of energy. There are three attunements to become a Master and one more to become a Master Teacher. It's funny to me that we are called "Masters," because all of the Reiki Masters that I have met would tell you that they have little to do with the healings. They are just a conduit for the energy to flow through. My healings became more powerful as I cleared my channel, including quieting my ego, and I simply got out of the way and let the energy flow.

The energy directs itself. Even though I might put my hands on someone's heart to clear a physical blockage there, the energy might flow into another part of their body to ease the emotional heartache that caused the physical issue. It is typical for the Reiki practitioner to put their hands on one part of someone's body, only to have that person report feeling the energy going someplace else.

My life began to change swiftly after my first attunement. I believe it accelerated the clearing of my channel.

Feeling this energy for the first time was exhilarating. I felt like I was feeling a part of God's energy and it made me feel completely connected to Him, so I knew I could never again doubt that God existed. Rather than feel empowered by this energy from God, which I did eventually, I immediately felt completely humbled. I knew I was a part of something very huge, powerful and overwhelmingly loving. I cried tears of joy.

Along with the physical, emotional, and mental healing ability that I received, I also seemed to be gifted with the ability to awaken people spiritually. I wasn't trying to, but it seemed that the lives of many folks I encountered after my Reiki training were shaken up, thereby creating the potential for a greater connection to the Divine. It fits, then, that the attunement to Reiki energy propelled me into writing a book for those who were awakening spiritually.

As I began working with more people and teaching more, it seemed to help when I shared my personal stories. I revealed the good and the bad, the easy and the hard. For some it prepared them for what was to come and for others it validated what they were already experiencing; it comforted them to know that they were not alone.

Reiki is not at all necessary for spiritual awakening, but it was a major factor in my awakening.

Operator's Guide

Some of you have begun to experience the phenomena I describe. Others will soon. I hope my story will help you make better sense of your experiences. I hope this information serves as a guide for your journey to some places that you may not yet know exist.

I trust this book will remind you that:

- You have vast resources available to you
- You are part of a divine plan
- You have a beautiful purpose in life
- You are a master at manifesting what you desire
- You are a healer with tremendous capacity to heal yourself and others
- You are capable of interacting with non-physical presences around you
- You are completely safe, as long as you continually align yourself with love and light

- You are an energetic being capable of detecting, embracing, and dissolving subtle energies that are ever-present around you
- You can connect with your intuition, your higher self and your guidance whenever you need help
- You are a being of great love and joy
- You can use your experiences to clear your channel (your physical, emotional, mental and spiritual bodies) to allow more light and love to flow through you to further enhance your abilities
- You are more POWERFUL than you ever imagined.

I pray that this knowledge will propel you to step forward into who you truly are, that you will use this energy in the best possible way, and you will find the courage to do what you came here to do.

Chapter 1

Energy

Can You Feel It?

Let's start with a primer on energy. Most of us don't think in terms of energy, yet energy is all around us. It makes up everything. More and more people are giving themselves permission to feel the energy, but they tend to brush it off as an itch, a cobweb, depression, anxiety, Restless Leg Syndrome, a joint pain, or some kind of nervous problem. We are not educated to be aware of the energy that is all around us and flowing through us. The purpose of this chapter is to make you more aware of this energy and of the energy experiences you're already having.

I hope to expand your awareness to the world of energy so that more of these experiences will begin to occur in your life. And they will. Once you become open, you free Spirit to operate more fully in your life. Remember that you *are* energy in your purest form. You know what energy is and how to use it. Tuning into the energy around you allows you to do many things, including:

- Increase your intuition
- Work more closely and consciously with your guides and Angels
- Heal yourself and others
- Benefit more fully from environmental energy shifts
- Keep your body and energy fields balanced
- Make contact with loved ones and helpers on the Other Side

How to Feel Energy

You can begin to feel the energy of something by putting your hand just above it. Plants, and especially flowers, give off a lot of energy, so try running your hand about one inch above a flower and see if you can feel a change in the sensation in the palm of your hand. You may feel heat, a magnetic sensation of pulling and pushing, coolness, a vibration or a sense of thickness. Close your eyes and put all of your attention into your palm. I have an orchid I use to help people feel energy. The energy of my orchid is greatest when it has buds, just before it flowers.

Another experiment is to bring your palms close to each other, and then begin to move them in-and-out, closer and farther away from each other. You may feel a magnetic pushing-and-pulling sensation. See how far out you can move your hands while still feeling the energy. Then try putting your palm to someone else's palm. Hold your palm about an inch from theirs and see if you can feel anything. Swirl your hand in a circle in front of theirs (or your own) and feel the energy shifting. Next have your partner lie down and run your palm above their body from head to toe. Move slowly and focus on your palm. Branch out from there to other people and even objects.

You can also feel the energy of something that is not physically present. Energy healers do this when they do distant healing. One day, Will Linville said to me, "I want you to hold your current financial situation in your hands." I held my hands out in front of me as if I was holding a ball, with my palms facing each other. I could feel energy in my hands. The energy then began pushing my hands further apart and I remarked on it to Will. He said, "That is because the Universe wants you to have everything you want. It is we who limit it." What an empowering and exciting concept.

When I work with Reiki, I feel the energy coming from my hands, and from the person I'm working on, as heat. I've always felt injury as heat —not just where there's swelling (which is typically hot), but any injury. I've always put my hands on my own injury, as most of us do, because something about that action makes it feel better. I thought everyone felt injuries as heat and I was surprised to learn that they didn't. It never even occurred to me to say anything about it because it seemed so normal.

Anyone can cultivate sensitivity to energy. It is less about thinking and more about feeling. It may feel like heat, or a prickly feeling, or a pins-

and-needles feeling. The next time you or someone you know has pain or an injury, ask if you can put your palm directly on or above the area and see what you can feel. Focus your attention on your palm. You may or may not feel anything the first time. Just keep trying, and pay careful attention to any sensations. The mind tends to dismiss these feelings as "imagination." It's best if you can take a minute before you try to feel the energy. Sit quietly and take some deep breaths. Then tell your conscious mind to step aside, and tell your intuitive mind to take charge. Imagine your conscious mind sitting in a big armchair, with a footstool.

At times, you may feel as if someone is gently stroking your cheek, but there's no one there. Or maybe a strand of hair brushed over your cheek, but when you lift your hand to remove it, there's no hair there. You may, in fact, be connecting with the energy around you. I found out early on that just by asking Spirit to touch me and to allow me to feel it, that I could increase those experiences. They would happen all the time.

Sit quietly for a moment and ask to feel an Angelic presence. What do you feel? Pay attention especially to your face or any other bare skin.

These sensations can be very minimal in the beginning. For me, all I had to do was acknowledge the *possibility* that it was Spirit in order to increase the intensity of the experiences. Then, especially when I was upset, I would ask Spirit to be around me, and I felt this wonderfully warm, comforting energy surrounding me. It reminded me that Spirit was always there—even when I could not feel a presence. Just ask for what you want, and know that even though you may not be able to feel it, it's happening. It might not happen right away, but with time, you'll feel it.

In the beginning, I could only feel Spirit at nighttime or when it was quiet. It helped if I was alone and without a lot of other sensory input. It was harder to isolate that feeling in the midst of others. Now, if I can't feel my Angels, I just ask for them and I can feel their energy. Meditation can help to increase awareness of these experiences. It's good to request that Jesus, another Avatar or an Angel be present to supervise what's happening. In this way you can alleviate fear and anxiety, knowing that what is happening is in your highest good and the highest good of all. If you ever feel any doubt, just state aloud: "If this is not in the highest good, let it stop.

Early on, before I'd had much experience with energy and Spirit, I performed an experiment. I was listening to a Christian radio station, and there was a pastor who came on twice a week, with a short message. On this morning, he was speaking about filling up with the Holy Spirit. He said that we fill up with many things each day, and we need to make sure that one of them is the Holy Spirit. That was great, but I had no idea how to do that. I thought, well, in church you put your hands up to show that you surrender to God. Maybe that was a way to do it.

I focused on filling up with energy the whole day and faced one palm up whenever I could. By the end of the day, I had a red circle in the center of my palm. I had done it! It was that easy! I finally had the concrete proof that my rational mind had been wanting.

Vibrations in the Night
You may experience various sensations, like vibrations or warmth and calm during the quiet hours of the night. You may associate some of these feelings with anxiety because they're unfamiliar. I began feeling vibrations in my body that would wake me from sleeping.

Julie talks about knowing who is around her by the difference in vibration. For instance, Archangel Michael feels very warm, and she actually starts sweating when he is around. Jesus feels intense and loving. I don't always know whose vibration I am feeling, initially. Eventually, though, they give me enough information to figure it out.

The vibrations started out small. There was a rock quarry on a nearby mountain, and I just assumed I was feeling the blasting from the quarry. I would ask Frank the next morning if he'd felt it and, of course, he hadn't because it wasn't the blasting that I was feeling. It wasn't until I began feeling these vibrations in just one part of my body, and they became more intense and occurred during the day and at work, that I realized that it wasn't the quarry! I think it was my own vibration increasing. It was very low level; just enough to wake me up. Other times I would feel the chi moving in or releasing from my body. In our culture, we use the word "energy," but other cultures use the words "chi," "ki" or "prana" to describe the same thing.

As things began to intensify, I'd begin to feel a buzzing in the middle of the night. It was stronger than the little vibrations, and sometimes it would buzz me awake. My guides seemed to use the buzzing when they wanted to wake me up to show me something, like the number on the clock or if they wanted me to meditate. If I focused on the physical feeling of energy during meditation, just quietly observing my bodily sensations, it was a great way to get me out of my mind. It was especially helpful when I felt like my mind wouldn't settle down. It prolonged my ability to sit quietly. The meditations following the buzzing were always more intensified, as I could feel the energy all around me, and I could feel Spirit touching me.

When I first started meditating, I never felt anything. I was just trying to have longer periods of quiet. But one night I felt like there was a ball of energy swirling around underneath my chin. I used to meditate slouched over. I knew that you always saw pictures of people meditating sitting up super-straight, but it was the middle of the night, for goodness sake! I was tired! I figured I could be quiet slouched over, easier than I could sitting up straight (and maybe I could sneak in a little sleep at the same time).

A night or two later, I felt a ball of energy at my chin. It was small and it didn't last long. The next night it was back again and I started asking, "Why are you there? What are you trying to show me?" It felt like it was pushing up against my chin, so I lifted my chin up and the pushing-up-feeling stopped, but the energy stayed.

Over the course of the next few nights, the swirling ball, as I called it, kept coming back and showing me how I should be meditating! One night it centered on my back, and I knew to sit up straight. I've come to understand the posture while meditating to be similar to an antenna. A straighter antenna would allow for a clearer connection. Another night, there was a vibration at my lips and I knew my guide was telling me to breathe in through my nose and out through my mouth. I still hate this one because it takes too much conscious thought at a time when I am barely awake, so sometimes I do it and sometimes I don't. I received little reminders over the next few weeks when I would begin to slouch or drop my chin. Spirit was teaching me how to meditate.

Head Rocking

As time went on, other things began to happen during meditation. One night I felt a gentle rocking. Initially, it takes a very relaxed body and an attitude of allowing, to be able to feel that Spirit is trying to move you physically. It requires an openness to move where Spirit wants you to be.

I relaxed my head and neck and just let it go where it wanted and it began to rock back and forth. The first night it lasted for a couple of minutes. The next night it lasted 15 minutes and on the next it lasted 30 minutes. I periodically stopped my head, to make sure that I wasn't creating the rocking, but I still felt the sensation. On the other hand, when Spirit stopped the rocking, it stopped gently, but abruptly. This rocking went on for many months. It happens rarely now, but it still happens.

Andrea began to have the experience just after me, which was comforting for both of us. Since then, we have become bolder in sharing our experiences with each other and with other people, which allowed us to discover that other people experienced this, too. Most attributed it to a neurological problem. Julie told us that it's an attunement—perhaps to another level of vibration. She also said that Spirit is literally rocking our heads. She said that they have one hand on the back of our heads and one at our foreheads. I think if I'd known that it meant Spirit was actually standing right there, I would've been fearful. I was so comfortable with the rocking by the time I learned it was them, that I wasn't afraid.

One night I was told by Spirit that things were going to be a little bit different during that night's meditation: I received the word "dish" with the image of a satellite dish. My head began to move slowly in a big circle. This movement lasted quite awhile and, as usual, I stopped the movement periodically to make sure that Spirit still wanted me to move that way. True to form, Spirit stopped it gently, but abruptly, and there was no mistaking that it was done. The whole time, I was surrounded by a warm, loving vibration. It felt like Spirit was aligning my energy.

These sensations were very subtle. The key was to allow and to be very relaxed so that I could feel where Spirit was urging me to move. My hope is that in knowing these things happen, it will speed up the process for others.

Some people told me they believed they were experiencing early symptoms of multiple sclerosis or Parkinson's disease. It's amazing how our first thought upon feeling something new or different is that it must be a disease or something must be wrong. Consider when you feel these sensations, that it's actually an expansion. You are expanding into all that you truly are. Relax and enjoy it, and you'll probably be able to reduce or eliminate the feeling of anxiety.

Chakra Clearings

For a couple of nights I heard a hum or buzzing sound that I could only hear when my head was in a specific spot. If I moved my head even a little, the sound went away. I assumed that there was a specific vibration of energy that resulted in a sound when I aligned with it. On other nights there was no sound, but I saw geometric shapes moving incredibly fast downward. It was hard to see them clearly because they were moving so fast. It felt like I was being downloaded with information, yet I had no idea what it was.

This downloading continues to happen periodically. Will said that I'm now at a point where I can see inside these shapes to see what they carry. I have tried a couple times—but no luck so far.

Next, I'd feel this vibration or ball of energy moving at each of my chakras. The chakras are energy centers on the body where energy can enter and exit the body more easily. The seven main chakras run along the spine. Between the legs is the root chakra, below the belly button is the sacral, above the belly button is the solar plexus, at the heart level is the heart chakra, at the throat is the throat chakra, between the eyes at the bottom of your forehead is the third eye and on the top of the head is the crown chakra. I began to feel Spirit "playing" at these centers. I felt it mostly at the throat, the third eye and the crown.

One day after yoga, Julie and I were sitting at the coffee house and I said, "I feel them right now, right here" pointing to my neck area. She smiled and laughed a little—this was after she could see Spirit—and said, "Spirit is touching you there." She said that "he" was standing in the corner and had just walked over and touched me there.

She said, "He's talking to you— can you hear it?" But I couldn't. This was a big source of frustration for me—knowing they were talking, but not being able to hear it like a voice, even though I was receiving a knowing of some information.

There were times when I would ask repeatedly, "Show me that you're here." If I began to feel like I was about to see something, I might become scared. I realize now that Spirit wouldn't show itself to me while I was still afraid. I know now that it's starting to come, because I can see vague shadows moving around. I know it will become clearer as I'm ready for it.

Don't be afraid. Your Angels and Guides won't try to scare you. They'll ease you in as you're ready for them. If you have no fears, it will happen more quickly. Spirit is all good and all loving and is there only to guide and help you. Ask to lift any fears you might have about developing a deeper connection.

Seeing Colors

I might just be sitting and eating lunch with a friend, when suddenly I'll feel a vibration in my body or hear a tone in my ear. Then I know that Spirit is trying to get my attention. I'll look up and I might see a block of green or red color on the wall, just off to one side, in my peripheral vision.

I used to see these colors and dismiss them as a visual disturbance of some sort—like when you look at something and then look at a blank wall and see an afterimage. I played around with it and I became convinced that the block of color was definitely there.

Once I saw a bright neon-looking red light, and it stayed with me even when I got up and went into the bathroom across the hall. It was there on the wall, in the bathroom.

I was starting to catch on, so I asked, "Are you an Angel?" The lights flickered.

Lights tend to flicker around me a lot, and I have come to regard it as a way that Spirit lets me know that a presence is there, or confirms something I was talking or thinking about. I'd point it out to people who then began to recognize that the lights *did* flicker a lot when they were with me.

They'd say to me, "Did you do that?!"

I'd just say, "No, that's the Angels."

So I called Julie and told her that I had this red neon-looking light with me and I had asked for confirmation that it was an Angel and I received one through the lights. She said, "Yes, they are confirming your confirmation! It's Ariel. She's not the only one around you right now, but she's the one you're seeing."

Each time these Angels showed up as colors when I was with someone else, I assumed the Angels were there for me. Then I began to notice that they kept showing up with the same couple of people. One day it dawned on me that I was seeing *their* Guides. They were actually there for them!

I began to perceive Archangel Michael's blue light. Twice he appeared in my car, and then many times at home and in my office. Now he's a frequent visitor. One of the first times I experienced Michael, I was in my car at night and I saw his blue glow and felt a light touch on my cheek. I said, "Michael, is that you?" The touch intensified and stayed for a bit. Michael often appears as a quick flash of blue, while Ariel and Raphael have larger blocks of color and appear stationary.

I was disappointed that I was seeing them as color and feeling them as vibration instead of seeing wings and flowing robes. Then I realized that I was most likely seeing them in their most pure form. The wings and robes represent man's depiction of them and not their true state. Similarly, the experience of being touched by them, or hearing them, is also a representation of an energetic connection. The colors indicate the frequencies of their vibrations.

Doreen Virtue's book, *Angels and Ascended Masters: A guide to working with and healing with Divinities and Deities*[1] can help you identify who is with you when you see a particular color. She provides information about each Ascended Master and Angel, along with their colors.

When you see color around a person, you are seeing their aura. This is their energy. It may appear at first as simply a white glow around the person. But with time and practice, you may begin to see neon colors as well. With more time, you may see it extend farther out from the person in layers.

Initially, auras are easiest to see when someone is standing in front of a light colored wall. Let your eyes go out of focus as you look at him. You'll probably first see a white glow around his shoulders and head. This is his energy field. There are several books available to help you learn to see auras.

You may find that you are better at one mode of perceiving energy than another. For instance, you may be able to feel the energy around a person better than you can see their aura. This is normal. Each way has its advantages, but none is better than another.

More Vibrations

Now I'm often aware that a physical vibration is with me. It seems to come in times when comfort is needed, or when I need to pay special attention to what's happening around me. Sometimes it reminds me that an opportunity is being presented, so I can trust it and lean on Spirit to guide me about what to do next. However, I am always aware that I have freewill and am therefore free to make my own choices.

As you become more accustomed to feeling energy, put your palms out as you go to different places, to feel the energy. As time goes on, you may be able to feel it in your face, and then your body. People are most likely reading this kind of energy when they say, "I don't like the feel of this place," or "He gives me bad vibes."

We have not been encouraged to feel the energy. But I'm sure you can think of numerous occasions when you weren't comfortable with who you were with, or where you were, but couldn't explain why. Tap into it, and honor those feelings, because they are a very valuable resource.

As you get better at tuning in to your body, you may begin to experience energy both outside and inside of you. I can feel a flow through my body at times. When I'm doing energy work like Reiki, or Jin Shin Jyutsu, on myself, the feeling may be very pronounced.

I had a longstanding pain in my leg, from the auto accident. Lindy, my yoga instructor, tried to open up a flow in my leg with Jin Shin Jyutsu. At first I felt nothing (except the original pain) and then, as the flow opened, I felt a sensation of something flowing down my leg and out my foot. I finally felt a release of that old, chronic, debilitating pain.

Sometimes I experience a release of energy as a "bubbling" at the surface of my skin. It feels like a tiny muscle spasm. It's so easy to dismiss these sensations until we realize what they are.

I can concentrate on increasing the flow of blood and lymph and energy to an area where I have pain or discomfort and I can feel the flow returning to that area. When I work on others, I often feel a flow down my own legs and out my feet. This might be when I'm working on someone with Reiki or Integrated Energy Therapy (another vibration of energy healing). It tends to happen more when I'm in a group of people. I've been told that I'm clearing something from them through my body and that's exactly what it feels like.

Collective Consciousness

I distinctly remember the first time I saw energy, although I had no idea that's what it was. I was a young teen and it was a sunny day. I was on the bench during a softball game. I looked up and saw particles dancing around in the sky. You may have seen this, too. I looked in awe, wondering what they were. I could always see them if I looked for them, and sometimes if I didn't. I could see them easily if I looked up into the sky on a bright day, and let my eyes go slightly unfocused. It's become easier to see these particles, even when I'm not looking for them.

Some people say this is just energy, while Will said that these particles are mass consciousness or collective consciousness. What we're actually seeing is thought forms; thoughts that people have had. Either way, they are energy, and most would agree there is a collective consciousness that impacts us. The thought forms are all around us and they impact the way we think, feel and act. After learning about them, I made a conscious decision to disengage from the mass consciousness. That means that I no longer accept conventional wisdom as true for myself. That means not accepting things like "You're supposed to do it that way," "That causes cancer," "Everybody is like that," and "Diabetes runs in my family, so I'm sure I'll get it, too." Instead, I choose to create things in my life as I go along and as they fit my life.

Because thoughts have form, our thoughts matter. If you're constantly having negative thoughts, not only are you attracting those negative things toward you, but you're also adding negative thought forms to the collective consciousness. This negative energy sometimes gets released or transmuted through catastrophic events like hurricanes and tsunamis and also impacts individuals' behavior. Now imagine how an event like 9/11 impacts the collective consciousness as everyone falls into fear and all of that fear is sent out into the collective consciousness and hovers all around us. Imagine instead, if everyone reacted only with compassion and forgiveness and not fear. How different the collective consciousness would be. What kind of thoughts are you adding to the collective consciousness?

Becoming Empathic
You may have begun to recognize that you wake up light and happy some days and other days there's a heaviness that doesn't seem connected to specific events. You are being affected by the energy around you. I saw this in myself and I would've just thought that it was my varying moods, but Andrea and I began to notice that our feelings often matched. We

consciously noticed it on a day that we were feeling inexplicably giddy. Julie told us that the energy that day had a higher frequency vibration.

You may also be sensitive to the emotions of people around you. I now pick up on other people's sadness and anger. I also pick up on their happiness, but I'm more aware of the heavier emotions because I don't want them! More than once, I've felt overwhelmingly sad and I had absolutely no way to explain it. The first time I was aware of this happening, the sadness was so intense that it overwhelmed me. I was sitting at a soccer game fighting back tears, and I had no reason to cry. Frank and the kids wanted to know why I was so sad (and frankly, so did I). They kept thinking they must be the cause of it; they must have done something I wasn't telling them about. I eventually had to go off by myself and let it pass. Later, Will told me that I was actually running some of Frank's grief through me. His father died a couple months before; his grief was intense.

All thoughts and feelings are energy and energy exists all around you. So when you enter into someone else's aura by standing close to them, you can pick up on and experience their energy. Most people are walled off from this and don't experience it, but once you begin to open yourself up to energy, you may feel other people's emotions more than in the past.

Will told me that I needed to protect myself and make sure I'm only experiencing my own emotions and not other people's. (I talk more about protection in Chapter 12.) I have mixed feelings about protecting myself, because I would gladly experience an hour or even a day of intense sadness to help Frank clear some of his grief. I assume, though, that it should be possible to help people to clear their emotions without experiencing them myself. That's what I'll aim for.

When Frank was in the middle of the strongest part of his grief, it was difficult for me as well. I had my own grief over losing my very loving father-in-law, but then I also felt Frank's pain whenever I was around him. I also feel his anger and frustration. I try to recognize that they're not mine, so that I don't act on them. When you're feeling angry, it's natural to say, "Well then, I must be mad at you" and assign the cause to the person closest to you.

Once, I walked up to a friend who was in the middle of a divorce. He didn't want the divorce and it was tearing him up. As I approached him, I felt like I walked into a wall of depression; it wrenched my heart and knocked the wind out of me.

In another case, I was in a funeral home attending the wake of someone I did not know, but I knew his wife and daughter. Walking up to the receiving line, I was so overcome by sadness that my friend standing next to me in line asked if I needed to go sit down in the back.

The next day, I was extremely sad and kept seeing images of the wife and daughter in my head, so I assumed it was connected to them. Then my friend Tracy called and described the same feeling of sadness and the same knowing that it was tied to our mutual friends.

We have all had experiences where we have felt empathy for another person. But now I literally feel what that person is feeling, and it is stronger than ever before.

For Julie, the situation is often even more intense. She feels the pain of people even when she's not in close physical proximity to them. For example, I became extremely sad when I realized that I was going to have to go back to work after a leave of absence. I was mourning all the things that I was going to have to give up when I returned to work.

Julie felt my pain so intensely while she was driving that she needed to pull over to the side of the road to cry. She knew the emotion was mine, and called to see how I was doing. On the one hand, this ability seems like a curse, but what a blessing to be that connected to the people around you.

While it seems that more people are hooked on television than ever, some people are finding it harder and harder to watch the news and violent movies and to read violent and otherwise negative books because of increased empathic abilities. I noticed this first while watching the news. It made me sad and produced uncomfortable physical sensations that lasted after I turned the television off.

I felt that, by watching, I would end up contributing my negative emotions to the collective consciousness, so I stopped watching the news and I also stopped watching movies. I always loved action-adventure movies, but I recall being on a plane and watching one of those movies to entertain myself on the long flight. The bad guys began hurting the main character's girlfriend to get information out of him, and I literally couldn't breathe. My chest got tight and I felt sad, depressed and angry. That was the end; I entertained myself with a book for the rest of the flight!

Most people experienced this phenomenon following the events of 9/11. Watching television was crushing. Many people figured out that they needed to turn off the television and move on with their lives. There was a significant increase in the prescription of antidepressants following 9/11 and much of it was for regular folks who didn't directly know anyone who was killed or injured and only witnessed the events on television.

Because of this phenomenon, when I feel a certain emotion or react a certain way, I stop to make sure that it's related to something going on in my own life. For instance, if I'm feeling sad, I check to see if there is something that I'm sad about and question whether I'm just picking up on the energy of people around me.

You can experience energy in a variety of ways. You can feel it outside your body or inside your body. Notice what you're already feeling and ask yourself if you're feeling an energy or a Spirit presence around you? The more you begin to pay attention to these feelings, and allow that they might be energy and Spirit, the more you allow these experiences to grow, because Spirit knows you are listening for messages.

Also, the more you tune in to energy, the more sensitive you become to it. The more sensitive you become to it, the more you can be affected by it. This can be a good thing, or a bad thing, depending on the kind of energy that you're feeling. So it becomes important to know how to protect yourself, by using the energy clearing techniques in chapter 12.

Chapter 2

Building to Conscious Contact

Intuition and Beyond

The Spirit realm is constantly communicating with you. To some extent, your ability to receive the messages depends on the clearness of your channel (your body and energy field). It also depends on your readiness to receive them. I think of four types of messages:

- Concrete signs
- Body-level intuition
- Higher-level intuition
- Conscious contact

The type of message used depends on several factors, including: the openness of the receiver, the level of the Spirit giving the message and situational issues.

Concrete Signs

Concrete signs are exactly that—physical occurrences in the material world that Spirit shows you to convey a message. While you are clearing your channel, it will be easiest to receive information from your environment, so be alert to what's going on around you.

Devices, especially electronic ones, are one method that Spirit uses to communicate. As I mentioned before, lights flicker around me. It often happens when I enter a room. On several occasions, each light just ahead of me flickered as I walked down the hall at work. Most of the time, I think it is just letting me know Spirit is present. I smile or giggle and say a quiet "hello." But sometimes the light will flicker to get me to pay attention, or to confirm what I was saying or thinking.

A friend's son has a toy fire engine that rang its siren three separate times in my presence, when no one was touching it. She said it had never done that before and teased me. Given the make-up of the group of friends who were there that day, I think it was happening to let everyone know that Spirit is out there. It served to start a nice discussion on that topic.

One of my best friends, Karen, was very ill and we used to spend time discussing our views of the afterlife. She didn't believe in life after death, but I told her that she would be able to contact me after passing, and I expected her to do so.

She died a few weeks later. Three days after she died, I was lying in bed thinking of Karen when the light down the hall in my daughter's bedroom began to flicker crazily. I was flooded with a sense of her presence. The flickering stopped and I asked, "Karen, is that you?" The flickering started again and then quickly stopped, as if acknowledging my question. Message delivered! She had gotten through. I smiled smugly at the fact that I was right, because I knew she would have hated that. But I knew she was smiling, too. She has come back many times since then. Now that the painful part of my grief is resolved, I'm aware that she comes every time I talk to her, and I'm able to hear her responses.

My car radio got in on the act a few weeks before I received my first Reiki attunement. I had purchased a new-for-me car and was enjoying my forty-minute commute to-and-from work. But after a few weeks, the radio cut out. I felt angry as I played with the dial, looking for any station that might come in. The only station I could get was the Christian radio station. Now I was really mad! I wasn't listening to that stuff! Over the next week, I alternated between silence and the Christian station. By the end of the week, I wanted my station back, so I told Frank we had to get that car in for service! On Monday, when I went back to work, the reception was back and I enjoyed my old station. But about a week later, the same thing happened. By then I knew a few of the songs on the Christian station, so it wasn't as bad, but by the end of the week, I told Frank that we needed to get it fixed. Again, it fixed itself by Monday.

This continued for a couple months and I was beginning to enjoy the Christian station. There was a very positive vibration to the music. It simply felt good to listen to it. The radio was out on the week that led up to my Reiki Level 1 training and I took advantage of the opportunity to be silent in the car. Coming out of my class, I had a knowing that the radio would be back and stay back this time. It was no longer needed, because it had done its job of getting me to spend more time in quiet, to recognize that a Higher Power was around me and aware of me and to show that different music had different vibrations. It has, on occasion since then, gone out for a brief time to confirm something that I was thinking, but mostly it has worked fine.

Even the Dog

Even Willie, my big black mutt, got in on delivering a message from Spirit. I was sitting at my computer, writing and wondering whether I should be focused on getting my message out first and then go back and edit, or if I should try to make grammatical corrections as I went. At that moment, Willie walked up to me with a card in his mouth. Willie was known for grabbing anything he could and ripping it up. He *always* ran *away* from you when he found something, because he knew he wasn't supposed to have it. This time, though, he walked proudly up to me and let me take the card out of his mouth. It was an autism awareness flyer that said, "Step by step we'll find the missing pieces." I knew it was telling me not to worry about it—Spirit was with me and we'd figure it out as we went along.

Be alert to messages arriving in all kinds of ways. You can always find answers to your questions if you're open to it. Often the answers come in odd ways. For example, I have a teasing kind of way of interacting with good friends, and I'd been wondering whether I needed to change that—if I could! I'd been thinking about it a lot when I went on a business trip to Boston. As I was driving, I felt my head being turned to the side. I had had this experience before, so I knew it was Spirit showing me something, but I was driving, for Pete's sake!

So I said aloud, "Hello! I'm driving here! That may not matter to you, but it does to me!"

The distinct feeling that a set of hands was turning my head continued, so I said, "All right, but show me quickly!"

I turned my head just in time to see a billboard with huge words that said, "Free to be Witty." I laughed aloud as I thanked Spirit for the answer to my question!

Numbers

You have probably had the experience of seeing the same number over and over. You might be awakened at exactly the same time every night, or you might see it on the odometer in the car, or on license plates. This is very likely a message from your guidance realm. You can refer to Doreen Virtue and Lynnette Brown's book, *Angel Numbers: the angels explain the meaning of 111, 444 and other numbers in your life.* It can help you understand the messages that Spirit wants you to receive. Doreen Virtue gives the meanings for these numbers in her book. Watch how the numbers change to conform to what's happening in your life. For example, I kept being shown 555 (meaning: there is a big change coming). I had no idea what that might mean. Shortly thereafter, I took an unexpected leave of absence from work.

Then I went through a period when Spirit would wake me up with one of the several numbers that mean, "Get going, you have work to do." That was when I was procrastinating about writing this book. They appeared many nights in a row, to let me know that I was not just randomly waking up, but that they were doing it because they wanted me working. I would know they were there by a vibration at my neck—the chakra related to communication.

Sometimes they woke me up with what I call "The Buzz." It's a full-body quick jolt of energy that feels great, but is mildly startling. They seemed to use this approach when I was in a very deep sleep and only something drastic would do! Other times I would feel a steady rumble in my body, and I would feel certain that if I looked at the clock there'd be threes and fours, like 3:33 or 4:43, etc. From Doreen Virtue's book, I knew that these numbers relate to the Ascended Masters (threes) and the Angels (fours)—though they might mean something different for you. I would feel their energy throughout my body and they would confirm their presence through the numbers. I'd laugh and say, "That's great. I love that you're here, and I thank you for showing me, but, really, it's 3:43 in the morning—do you think we could do this later, when I'm awake?" I knew, though, that they were coming to me then because I needed to get quieter before I could experience them with more regularity during the day.

Don't dismiss nighttime wakings. Look a little closer to see if you're being sent a message. Do you always awake at the same time? Are the final two digits always the same? How did you come to be awake? What happened to wake you? Are you feeling a gentle urging to do something, like meditating, writing or painting? Since you're more divinely inspired at these times, it's a good time to get up and do the task, even though you probably want to sleep.

When I'm sleeping too deeply to be awakened on my own, Spirit will use what is around me, like the door to the adjoining room blowing open, or Frank and the dogs rolling around and waking me up. Then I'd check the clock and I'd have my number to confirm that I was awakened for a purpose.

The day after the first time I got over my resistance and got up in the middle of the night to write, I was excited and pleased with myself. Later, I was driving down to Virginia from New Jersey (a five-hour drive) and I said to Spirit, "Are you pleased with me? I want to know that you are pleased." Then I kept seeing the same number on license plates. At one point the two cars on either side just ahead of me had the same number in their plates. At the next Rest Stop, I looked up the number (that I have forgotten now) and it said something about being pleased with yourself for a job well done. I said, "Yes, I am pleased, but that's not what I'm asking. I want to know that *you* are pleased. I want to see 777 from *you*." I knew that 777 had to do with congratulations for a job well done.

I made it down to Virginia without my sevens and reiterated my request on my way back up. I made it almost all the way home when I heard a loud constant tone in my ear. I knew this meant that Spirit was near and there was something for me to take note of. I looked all around outside as I was driving and didn't see anything. The tone persisted, so I continued looking. Then I checked the interior of the car and finally, on the odometer, there appeared three sevens in a row. I laughed out loud and thanked Spirit for humoring me. They had gotten it under the wire, just before I arrived home.

On this same drive home, I told Spirit that I would leave the radio off, so if they wanted to give me some information, I would be receptive, or if there was value in just being quiet, that was okay, too. Midway through the drive, I stopped at a Rest Stop for lunch and continued eating as I got back in the car. Distracted by the food, I forgot my promise and put the radio on. Then I kept seeing 140 on license plates and on my odometer. I stopped my car and pulled out the number book. Sure enough, 140 means: "Take time for quiet contemplation and meditation." I was floored. They reminded me of my promise. I laughed and turned the radio off.

Make no mistake about it. They know everything and they are there all the time.

And yes, there was a time when they were using numbers so much to communicate with me, that I always had the book nearby. Now it sits in my office and I use it rarely, since most of what I get now comes through higher level intuition.

When is a Billboard Just a Billboard?

Frank listens to all of my stories. Although he's a true believer in things spiritual, he thinks I get carried away with interpreting everything as a message. He'll ask, "When is a number just a number?" It's a great question. I think the answer is that you just know. When the same number appears repeatedly, or when further events play out to show you that your "hunch" was right, you realize that divine guidance was involved.

As you become more in tune with Spirit, more quiet within yourself and more observant of the world around you, you just know that the message is for you. The intuitive voice or feeling becomes stronger; the number is paired with being drawn to look at it at that moment; and there's a feeling of presence. I don't always look at a number and think it's a message, and I had *never* before thought that a billboard was trying to tell me something.

As your channel clears and your abilities grow, the message becomes so clear, whether through an inner voice, a vision, a feeling, or a knowing, that there is no doubt that the message was divinely given.

There are virtually always concrete explanations for what you may believe to be spiritually based. You are free to take whatever viewpoint you desire. I chose the concrete route most of my life. Having a concrete explanation gives the people who are not open to spiritual possibilities answers that do not threaten their belief systems. I have also met plenty of people who are spiritually oriented who have not had these kinds of experiences, and even some of those people are skeptical about many of the experiences I describe. These experiences are not a part of their path and their way of understanding. What a beautiful thing that there are so many paths.

Body-Level Intuition

I think of this "gut-level" intuition as *body* level, because I feel it as a tightening in my abdomen (third chakra area) or chest (fourth chakra). This is the level people are talking about when they say, "I have a hunch."

Will (my psychic friend) showed Frank that he already knew the answers to some business decisions by having Frank attend to how his body felt. Will said, "Now think about using that second lawyer for that deal. How does that feel in your body?" If Frank's abdomen or chest tightened up, that was a clear sign that Frank shouldn't trust the guy. Will coached Frank to first recognize his own feelings, and then pay attention to them, and to *honor* them, because the information was valuable! Our bodies will tell us what the truth is; all we need to do is pay attention.

Body Messages

Most of my early messages came in the form of pain. I remember leaving my daughter at gymnastics one day and, as I was about to drive around the corner of the building, I felt a sudden sharp pain in my right foot. It was so intense that I had to take my foot off the gas pedal. The next moment, a car came around the corner from the other direction, cutting way too tightly. Had I not raised my foot, I would've been hit by the other car. I immediately thanked Spirit for warning me— but then I asked Spirit to just *tell* me.

Then my knees became targets for pain-based messages. One of my teachers, Joy Gardner, relates the knees to responsibility. I had taken on too much responsibility at that point and I knew I needed to slow down, but I didn't believe that I could. I had a volunteer leadership position that consumed a lot of time, in addition to my full time work and my family, so I felt like I just needed to see it through.

I started saying, "Okay, okay, I'll slow down, but I just can't do it yet." Then I tore the meniscus in my knee and I had no choice, I had to slow down. At that time, I didn't know we have the potential to heal ourselves, so I had surgery about four months later—when I finally felt I had the time.

Next, knee pain came to show me that there was a disconnection at work. Even though I was still saying, "I love my job," it really had changed. I liked my job, but I no longer loved it. Pain in the knees is often connected with not stepping forward into what comes next. So I was holding back and not stepping forward. I wasn't even aware that I needed to make a change. Two years later, I tore the other knee. I believe that tear was related to worrying about my next steps. First there was fear over the potential judgment of my family for writing this book and second . . . what would society think? Clearly I feared the judgment of others and needed to work through that.

When I was considering taking a leave of absence from work to help take care of several family members who were ill, I began to experience neck pain. I knew then that I would not be able to take care of myself while trying to manage everyone else, so the decision to leave work became an easy one. The decision required careful listening to my body and recognizing what that pain was telling me (and listening to Frank, who really thought it would be best to take the break!).

Why is Your Pain Here?

I know now that the physical pain that I carried for *twenty-two* years following my car accident was to wake me up to the Spirit world and my divine life purpose. As soon as I figured that out, the pain eased. It was as simple as that. Had I known what the pain was about, I would not have waited twenty-two years to make a change! I tried everything that western medicine had to offer, to make it go away and nothing made a lasting change. How different things might be for all of humanity if there was a question on the doctor's history form that asked, "What is this pain here to tell you?"

I have put this question to a number of people. I was so nervous the first time I asked. I was being guided to ask, but I was still afraid he would think I was nuts. I was giving Reiki to Rick, an acquaintance who had been in a car accident ten years previously and was still experiencing neck and back pain. His friend, who had been driving at the time, had been drunk. Rick said that his friend was still involved in self-destructive behaviors. When I asked Rick why the pain was still with him—what it was trying to tell him—he responded without hesitation.

"If I'm still experiencing the consequences from the accident, then maybe my friend will feel a sense of responsibility and question his behaviors in life." We agreed that plan wasn't working and it was time to free himself from the accident.

Rick didn't say, "Well, this is pinched and that is swollen." He knew the underlying reason. I was amazed and thanked Spirit for pushing me to speak.

I put that question to you now. Consider every problem that you have. Consider every pain, every illness, every disease. Why are they here? What are they trying to tell you? If you look underneath, you will probably be surprised that you already know some of the answers. If you don't know, put the question to Spirit and your higher self. You may get lucky and be told or shown the answer immediately. Or, if you are like me, a series of experiences will follow that will lead you to the answer. You have to figure out what they mean or the experiences will continue. Then, if you'd like the issue to change, you need to focus on changing what they show you.

In trying to find the messages behind your pain, illness or disease, look hard at your thoughts and behaviors. Consider how other people would describe you. Sometimes they can view you more objectively because they are not emotionally attached to the behaviors. Would they say something like, "She tries too hard." "He worries too much." "She is so stressed." "That relationship is not working." "He would be so much happier if he'd pursue his dream of . . . . "

They may see the bigger picture better than you can. On the other hand, don't give your power away and blindly follow what others say. Just because they were accurate in the past doesn't mean they are right this time. Spend lots of time in silence and ask that the issue be revealed to you.

Sometimes the issues appear to be good things. I was proud that I planned so much and focused on getting things done. But I was limiting what the Universe could show me because I was too busy to listen. I tried to push the rock uphill, operating on my own. In reality, I could have completed so much more if I slowed down and listened to Spirit and to my own intuition.

Notice the behaviors in others that bother you. Sometimes we serve as mirrors for each other, reflecting back what we don't like about ourselves. Look at what annoys you in others and ask, "What is there for me to learn here?" "How do I need to change myself?"

Higher Level Intuition

Higher-level intuition is based at the sixth chakra (the "third-eye," at the center of the forehead). This chakra opens as you elevate your vibration and become more attuned to the spiritual world. Then you truly do become a Clear Channel. The prefix "clair" means "clear" in French, and by clearing your channel, you open up to the four "clairs:" clairvoyance, clairaudience, claircognizance and clairsentience.

- Clairvoyance (clear vision) allows you to see internal images, dream images and external phenomena such as auras and angelic energies.
- Clairaudience (clear hearing) enables you to hear the voice of Spirit and other spirits and your higher self. Some experience the voice as if it were coming from an external source, but most people experience it as an inner voice that is distinct from their own thoughts.
- Claircognizance (clear knowing) is a clear, strong knowing of information. This may come through dreams or meditation or visions and spontaneous insight.
- Clairsentience (clear feeling) is the ability to receive non-physical touch or sensations from the spirit world, and being able to feel the vibrations of people and things.

Experiences with the clairs grow in frequency and depth over time, as you seek to cultivate them.

By contrast, "gut-level or lower chakra intuition, discussed previously, comes as a more generalized feeling of tightening or pain in one of the lower chakras.

Whispered Messages

We're receiving messages all the time, even when we don't realize it. Looking back, I can see a couple of simple ways that Spirit was getting through, even in my earlier years. I learned in the last few years that two of my guides are named Mary and Michael. My son's name is Eric Michael and my daughter's name is Molly. Molly is a derivative of Mary. Coincidence? Perhaps. I think that it's also likely that I was tapping into my guides on some unconscious level, or that Spirit was having fun whispering their names in my ear!

Apparently they were also whispering into my mom's ear. My middle name is Joy. Two of the Angels that guide me are Gabriel and Raphael— the Angels of joy. I was told that Spirit was telling me to "be yellow." Then I learned that yellow is the color for—you guessed it—joy!

These are just some little ways that Spirit was at work in my early life. It confirms that God really *is* in the details. If you look back, I'm sure you'll see a number of things that appeared messed up at the time, but now appear perfect; things that needed to happen to get you to the place you are today. One of the most seemingly terrible events of my life—being thrown out of a car and suffering tremendous pain for years—led me to my husband, my career and later into Reiki and into writing this book.

Listen Up

One of the first times I was aware of being guided by Spirit, I was sitting at a red light ready to cross a six lane highway on my way to a mall. A huge dump truck sat, also waiting, to my left, blocking my view of oncoming traffic. I heard, "Don't go."

"Why not?" I asked inside my head.

"Don't go." It repeated.

I thought to myself, "You're just being paranoid." The light was still red.

"Don't go."

Thinking this was now pretty comical, I said out loud, "Fine. Then I won't go. I'll just sit here." I took my hands off the wheel.

The light turned green. I sat. The dump truck to my left sounded his horn in one continuous blast, as a garbage truck came barreling through the red light on the highway.

My jaw dropped. Tears came to my eyes.

Realizing the enormity of what just happened, I slowly made it to the mall, repeating, "Thank you, thank you, thank you."

Meditations and Dreams

Guidance frequently comes from meditations and dreams. They may reflect anxieties and issues in your life or provide the answer to a current question. Meditation and sleep quiet the ego and allow for a greater connection with Spirit and your higher self.

Julie receives an enormous amount of guidance during meditation. (And now Andrea and I do, too.) She's often shown events that are coming into our lives and she receives answers to questions we pose. At one point, she became overwhelmed by all that she was shown and all that she had to do. Spirit said to her, "You haven't done it all by yourself up until now; what makes you think you'll be doing it alone in the future?" What a humbling yet reassuring message.

In the beginning, the messages Andrea and I received were more simplistic, while we were honing our skills, learning how to tune in. Andrea was worried about paying a bill and was waiting for an overdue check. As she sat quietly in meditation, she heard, "You already have the check." She stopped meditating and ran downstairs and was guided to look in a folder. There it was! So much had been going on when she received the check that she put it into a folder with all her other paperwork and forgot it was there. Maybe Spirit reminded her, or maybe meditation allowed her mind to become quiet enough to tap into information that she already knew.

Later, the information became deeper and very clear. One night while I was working on the chapter about Jesus, I sat up in bed to meditate. Suddenly I was flooded with information about Jesus' life. Will Linville would say that I was remembering what I already knew in a different realm or dimension.

Dreams tend to be much more symbolic than waking guidance.

In a dream, I woke up and discovered that I had a beard. I wasn't at all upset; I thought its rusty red color was beautiful. I laid there in bed quite comfortable and relaxed until I heard someone coming in downstairs. Then I hurried to the bathroom to shave off my beard that I loved, before anyone could see it, because I was embarrassed. Of course, I couldn't shave it off fast enough and the dream ended as my anxiety built with the person coming into the bathroom. The message was immediately clear. I knew the dream was telling me to be myself in front of others. I had this other side to me now and I had to be comfortable showing it because I love it, and I don't need to worry about how others might judge it.

Again, just like the billboard, I'm not aware of every dream having a message, but I am aware of having more purposeful dreams than ever before. The ones with messages tend to relate to a current issue, or they point in the direction I need to head next. They also feel very real.

Frank receives a lot of answers to questions at night. He just wakes up with the answer. This happened so frequently that they began taking advantage of it at work. During engineering brainstorming sessions, his co-workers would take a corner of the whiteboard and designate it as "Frank's Dream Corner." Anything they couldn't solve would go in that corner for Frank to sleep on. Most times, he'd have the answer by morning.

Finder's Keepers

I have deemed Frank the "Finder of Lost Things" because he has an uncanny ability to use his guidance to find things. His answers come in a variety of ways. Once he searched everywhere for his glasses. Then he heard in his head the squeak that our truck seat makes when you fold it up. He checked under the seat and there they were.

On another occasion, after he misplaced his checkbook, he thought he kept hearing "suitcase" in his mind, so he checked every suitcase and briefcase he could find. After a day or so he finally realized that he was actually hearing "bass case" and then he found his checkbook in his bass guitar case. He remembered that he took the checkbook out while he was playing and just tossed it in for safe-keeping. Frank is so good at finding things that Andrea will call up with a missing item and tell me to ask Frank to find it for her!

Tracy had an experience where the knowing or inner voice led her to check her phone. She had been having one of those really bad days where all she wanted was a hug. She was lying in bed thinking about the hug when she heard in her head, "Check the phone" repeated over and over.

She protested, "No, I don't want to check the phone. I'm in bed!" The voice didn't stop so she finally got up and checked her cell phone. There was a text from a friend saying that she had seen Tracy earlier in a group and she really wanted to hug her because it looked like she really needed a hug, but because of where Tracy was sitting, she didn't. Tracy smiled and went back to bed. She had gotten her hug and Spirit wanted her to know it.

Conscious Contact

Conscious contact is the high end of the intuition continuum. It is a term I use to describe how people like Julie and Will live their lives. They *always* see Spirit and they are in a continuous, open, conscious, clear dialogue with the energy all around them. They are consciously aware of the information constantly flowing in, which is why I call it **conscious** contact. For the rest of us (at least until the connection is developed), the guidance tends to be subtle and fairly unconscious or subconscious. Although I have only seen conscious contact in a few, it is an ability I believe we're all capable of.

Others have also used the term conscious contact, often in a slightly different way, including Bill W. in the eleventh step of Alcoholics Anonymous' 12-step program and in Wayne Dyer's books.

I had the privilege of being present and watching as Julie moved along the continuum into conscious contact. She would often take on a slightly spacey look. She'd drop her head slightly, her eyes would go out of focus and we'd know she wasn't totally attentive to the conversation. Initially, she'd pretend there was nothing going on because she was embarrassed by her inattention. But when Andrea and I caught on to what was happening, we'd make her tell us what she saw or heard. Sometimes it was as if she was watching a movie happening around us. More than once, I'd be speaking and she would be staring at Andrea. I'd wave my hands and say jokingly, "Hello, I'm over here!" Julie would say, "I know, but I'm watching what they're doing to her."

Sometimes Spirit would be telling her the background details related to our discussion. For instance, I might be telling her about a tough time my son, Eric, was having at school, and they'd be telling her why the circumstances were important for his soul growth or she'd be listening to my grandmother's advice for him from the Other Side. All this made for some fun conversations.

Now I sometimes find myself with my eyes a bit out of focus in conversations, as I tune in to the messages I'm receiving from Spirit about what that person is talking about. It feels like I'm going into another space of consciousness.

At dinner one night, the waiter walked over to me and reached in front of me to take my plate away. As he approached, Julie sat up straighter and looked mildly concerned. When he left, I asked her what was going on. She said, "As he reached toward you, I literally watched your energies blend and I felt protective of you." She continued, "I've been seeing this level of energy more and more around things and people, and I now more fully understand the concept of our being all one." She was seeing that we extend far beyond our physical bodies.

While in conversation with Will, it's not uncommon to hear him acknowledging Spirit as he talks. "Uh huh. Thank you." Sometimes he switches to directly address Spirit and tell Spirit what he needs them to do in that moment for a healing. "Release that. Clear that. Thank you."

Need-to-Know Basis

After the first draft review, I received guidance that I should stress the following: What you know at any given point is all you need to know. You do not need to have any additional information from Spirit because you are powerful in and of yourself. All Spirit provides is support. Don't get hung up on having a message channeled from Spirit, or a sign. You are okay and you can be successful without it. You were okay before you knew any of this existed. You still are.

This is extremely important because it is easy to hand over all your decision-making to someone you deem a clearer channel than yourself. It can be tempting to pick up the phone and call a psychic every time there's a major decision to make. But you don't need to do that. Listen within and watch for outer signs and you will have all the guidance you need. Use others for support and always gauge what they say by how it feels to you. If you disagree with what a guide says (yours or someone else's), you don't need to feel guilty about it. The choice is always yours.

And on a related point, if you decide to call on a psychic, don't simply accept what they say, especially if it is something you perceive to be negative. For instance, if they say that something is wrong with your liver, don't leave it there. Ask what you can do to change that. It's the same thing if there is an outcome predicted that you don't like. Remember, you have the power to change things in your life.

Developing a Clear Connection

Develop a routine of finding quiet time so you can be still enough to connect to Spirit and receive messages. You are never alone. Spirit is always there to guide and support you. You can trust in that. They're pleased when someone tries to gain a closer communication with them and with their own higher self.

Initially, it was very hard for me to sit quietly. I liked the continual monologue that went on in my head, planning my next steps. I felt like I was one-up on many people because I was so good at creating my endless lists of things to do. Boy, was I wrong!

After a while, I began to treasure and anticipate my quiet time. I couldn't wait to put the kids to sleep so I could sit quietly and see what Spirit had in store for me. I recognized that the calm that was developing in my life was in large part due to my time spent in meditation. When life gets too busy, one of the things I miss most is my quiet time.

My ability to receive guidance or to channel information from my higher self is beginning to grow. It's clearer to me now when it's coming from ego-based thoughts versus a higher place. Guidance has an insistence, and yet it's not emotional. There's a feeling of importance to the message. It often has a sense of authority, and there may be a repetition like, "Say this, say this" until I say it. More and more I hear the guidance clearly.

The guidance realm is any non-physical consciousness that provides us with support and clarity. This may include God, Angels, Avatars, Ascended Masters, our higher self and relatives who have passed and return to play a role in our evolution.

The messages you receive may not always be 100% accurate, especially initially. It took me a lot of time and frustration to realize this. It can be difficult to discern the difference between guidance and thoughts that are ego-based. Then, when a message does come through, it has to come through your human filter, so there's still room for misinterpretation.

Learn what your strongest source of guidance is and tune in to it more fully, but be alert to messages coming in other ways. My strongest modes are clairsentience (feeling) and claircognizance (knowing), but I also receive assistance through clairaudience (hearing) and clairvoyance (seeing or visions). Be aware that the mode can change over time. I receive messages through pain and numbers less frequently now that I am more receptive in other ways.

Be careful about messages from Spirit involving time or timing. Spirit is not very good with time, since they don't have a linear existence. "Soon" never meant to them what it meant to me! *My* "soon" meant tomorrow and *theirs* seemed to be at least two months.

Be careful not to judge someone else's guidance. I may receive direction about someone else's life, but it's better when they can receive their own guidance.

Sometimes No Sign is a Sign

Andrea's husband, Anthony, received an unsolicited call from a company, offering him a position. He was very excited because it looked like he was being handed a good position. He told them how much money he would need to make it worth his while for a longer commute, and then asked the Universe for a sign telling him whether he should take the new position or stay with his current job. The new company needed to make a quick decision, so when Anthony didn't receive a call in a couple of days, he knew he didn't get the job. He was disappointed—both that he didn't get the offer, and that he didn't receive a clear sign.

Andrea, Anthony, Frank and I were out to dinner when he gave us the update. I quietly told Spirit that if they wanted to use me as a channel to give Anthony some guidance, they could.

Shortly thereafter, the conversation turned back to Anthony and the job and signs or lack of them. I felt moved to tell Anthony, "but you *did* get a sign: You *didn't* get the offer. What more specific sign could you get than the Universe taking the need to make a decision away from you?"

I could see his disappointment and I could see that he wasn't buying what I was saying, so I dropped it. But I remained absolutely certain that he had manifested an unequivocal sign. I also knew I would have reacted the same way. I would have doubted my own power. It taught me a good lesson about stepping back, taking my ego out of it and seeing the bigger picture.

Tracy calls this being outside of someone else's tunnel. It's hard to see for yourself while you're in your own tunnel. In fact, I'm quite certain that I couldn't have learned this lesson if it was *my* tunnel because my ego would have blocked it.

Think how many times you have wished for something to happen or even asked for a sign and then it didn't happen and you were disappointed. Consider now that it didn't happen because it wasn't right for you, and that you actually did receive your sign. It's only we who put specific guidelines on what a sign needs to look like. Apparently our guidance realms have other ideas!

Let Go of the Ego

For some people, the thought of being divinely guided feels threatening. It certainly was for me! If my actions were divinely guided, I reasoned, then my successes were not my own. Spirit could have my failures, but I wanted the successes! When I finally got to the point of consciously receiving divine guidance through signs, messages and intuition, I realized that it took a lot of work and faith on my part, and the successes felt very much like my own. In fact, it was even more exciting because I learned how to tap into something even bigger than my little ego. I guess I shouldn't sell it short—it was probably a pretty big ego. My work in this process involved self-healing, surrendering, allowing, meditating and really tuning in to my inner and outer worlds.

If you are still uncomfortable with Spirit guiding you, you can relax because your higher self is also involved. Your higher self knows all the choices you made and all the goals you laid out for yourself before you incarnated. But also recognize that Spirit is guiding you, based on those initial plans. Spirit may know that your targeted spiritual goals are being thwarted by the more salient demands of the physical world.

For example, you may have wanted to help some group by saving up your money to fund a project. Instead, you find yourself buying a botox treatment, a fad diet or expensive clothes. We all can get side-tracked like this, but often the guidance can help remind us what we really want for our life. Now, you can use your free will and thwart those plans wherever and whenever you like. Be my guest or, rather, be *your* guest. But you'll have to answer to yourself for not doing what you wanted to. You'll probably want to immediately reincarnate to finish everything you missed.

Most people I talk to about this concept say, "No way! This is too hard. I'm not coming back for a long time, if ever! I'm hanging out in the spirit world for a while and taking a break." Your higher self will likely think otherwise. I figure the more I achieve on my Pre-Incarnation Checklist, the more time it will take my higher self to come up with a new plan and the more time I'll have to hang out with the Angels and rest! (I know I'm just fooling myself, since there is no concept of time on the Other Side, but it helps my human mind to think this way!)

Growing in Guidance

Be watchful of the way that guidance is coming to you and know that it will evolve over time. It will likely begin with concrete signs, then move to body-level intuition, then higher-level intuition and finally to conscious contact, with lots of overlap at all levels. Spirit will use any way they can to communicate with you and give you the guidance that you need and desire.

Chapter 3

Allowing and Prayer

Be Open

One of the most important practices to help clear your channel and enhance communication with other realms is simply to be open. Be open to the possibility of spiritual occurrences. It's that mustard seed of faith. You just have to have an open door that Spirit can use.

When your conscious mind always has to have a *concrete* reason for unusual occurrences, open yourself to the possibility that it could have been something else. Allow for that. This is a major step in becoming a Clear Channel. Make no judgments about what is happening and just let it be. You will see that your unexplainable occurrences and your "coincidences" will grow, and things will happen on a daily basis that do not have concrete explanations. You will begin to recognize what Spirit feels like as you become more attuned to the vibration. You will begin to remember. You will feel Spirit come and comfort you when you call, and your feeling of closeness to the Spirit world will grow.

Be Still

I think that meditation is an incredibly important part of helping us to move into our fullest potential as human beings, toward *Homo spiritus*. The Bible tells us, "Be still and know that I am God,"[1] because you need the quiet in order to hear Spirit. Spirit gradually slowed me down and

35

revealed itself step by step, allowing me to be able to feel Spirit and know what it was saying.

For years, I awoke in the middle of the night with my head racing with thoughts of what I was going to do the next day and what I was going to accomplish. Over time, I began to notice that I was being woken up and my head was no longer racing. It was calm and quiet. That was nice, but I wanted to be sleeping. I began to get a sense that I was supposed to meditate; I was intentionally being woken up for that purpose.

If I fought meditating, I would not be able to sleep for awhile. But if I sat up and meditated, even for just a few moments, then I could go back to sleep! But that meant I had to sit up. If I tried to lie there and say, "Okay, I'm meditating now," it wouldn't count. Something always seemed to keep me awake. But if I sat up, I would be okay! So I sat!

In the beginning, I could only sit for a few minutes and then my body would start fidgeting or I would start to fall asleep. My mind was rarely focused on nothing—which some say is necessary in meditation. It's not. What *is* necessary is starting and trying. Spirit will help you with the rest. Just be willing to try. Your mind will eventually quiet down. Just stick with it. My mind was constantly thinking and constantly planning. But I sat and tried anyway. I would meditate for five minutes if that was all I could do, but I would sit up every single time they woke me up because I knew I was not going to sleep otherwise.

I have heard it said that prayer is talking to God and meditation is listening for the response and I believe this is true. Even when you don't necessarily hear something, you're learning and growing and opening up to being able to hear those messages throughout the day. They're not necessarily verbal messages. Meditation allows you to tune into that inner knowing. Meditation opens you up and is well worth the time and sleep disruption! Allow yourself to be open to the counsel coming in through meditation.

You don't have to meditate in the middle of the night. That was my way; that was when I felt the most quiet and receptive. So I meditated for many, many months like that. It was typically five minutes at a clip. If I was really lucky I could make it to fifteen minutes. Some days my body would have too much energy and I really couldn't settle down to meditate much at all, but I'd try anyway. It got to the point where I loved that time;

it really helped to quiet my mind and open me up. It allowed Spirit to enter into my life more fully, and it helped me to be open to feeling Spirit in my life.

I speak with people who tell me that they are being woken up in the night, but they are afraid to sit up and try to meditate. For some, it is simply fear of the dark. Others know that someone or something is regularly waking them, and the thought of sitting in the dark with some unknown entity is frightening to them.

I ask people to try anything they can manage. If they absolutely cannot sit up at night, then I tell them at least to sit quietly for a few minutes during the day. Perhaps they could try first thing in the morning, while they are still very open and receptive. They could try sitting up at night and putting the light on. If they cannot sit up, then they could try lying there and setting their intent to be open. No matter what you try, ask that the fear be taken away and keep attempting to sit and meditate. I have no doubt that over time you will become less fearful and will be able to sit up and meditate effectively.

Watch Your Thoughts

I realize now that prayer is important. I don't, however, think that prayer has to start with a "Dear God" and end with an "Amen." I believe that every thought that you have, everything that you say is prayer. God wants to give you what you want and He doesn't just start listening when you say, "Okay, God, now I'm talking to you." No. He's listening all the time.

I think of Spirit as being genderless, and I think of God as genderless— possibly incorporating the energy of both genders—but it is easier to just say "He."

He is listening to everything. He is listening to your every thought. So if you put thoughts out there like, "I'm not going to do this well," or "I'm always in pain," or "Everybody hates me," you will begin to get or continue to have experiences that match that. Because that's what He believes you must want and He wants to give you everything you want.

You need to be very careful in controlling your thoughts and watching your every thought. For example, I was always very self-deprecating and I would pick on things about myself, even though I liked me very much! That was just my style. I had to learn to watch that tendency and change it.

It's a very interesting exercise when you begin to look at your every thought. We have a lot of thoughts about things that we really don't want to happen. As you begin to think of thought as prayer, it becomes very evident that most of us need to shift our thinking. If we think of every action, idea, thought, and word as prayer, then we begin to see a shift in all our behavior and in the world around us.

Just allow those negative thoughts when they come, but don't attach any emotion or judgment to them. Then begin to cancel them out. I practice canceling with people around me. When someone says to me, "He's always like that," I say, "Yes, but he's changing."

When they say, "I'm always in pain," I say, "But it's letting up now, it's going to get better."

When they say, "I'm so tired of being depressed," I say, "Yes, but you're changing some of those behaviors now that keep you depressed."

I practice canceling those thoughts out and begin to shift myself and others into a more positive way of thinking. Because, as Kathryn Rose, my Reiki Master, pointed out, "You will get what you believe."

Before I knew much about energy healing and Spirit, I was drawn to a holistic fair in the next town. There I met Kathryn, who had an information table about her services and was giving energy sessions. I was always looking for something to relieve the pain I had been experiencing for twenty-two years, since the accident. Kathryn simply put her hands on my shoulder and neck. After a few minutes, she said, "There, something just moved." I didn't feel anything, but strangely, I believed her and felt better. I said, "I just hope it sticks."

Kathryn said, "What do you mean?"

I said, "I have had so many experiences of getting relief, only to have the pain return."

She squatted down and looked me in the eye as I sat in the chair and she said, "Then you need to change your belief."

I had never heard this concept before. If I did, it probably just got put in the platitude pile. But this time I heard it differently and I believed. Something about Kathryn looking into my eyes and saying, "You need to believe that this pain is not coming back, because you will get what you believe," was very powerful for me. So I tried with all my heart to believe that this pain was not coming back and as I went forward the pain slowly lifted. I signed up for a Reiki class with Kathryn that June, and my life has not been the same. With Kathryn's help, I allowed for something different, and something different presented.

What do you believe? Are you ready to allow for something different? Do you believe that you have the power to create something different?

"Lord, Bless this Garbage"

Early in my awakening process, I met a high school friend for lunch. Mark was recovering from an illness. He walked into the restaurant wearing a very small pouch around his neck. I asked about the pouch and he said, "It contains herbs to make me stronger." That was an odd concept for me. I teased him a little bit, but I was curious. He said, "Well, you can even just bless things and they will be better for you." This was going too far! I looked at him unbelievingly.

I had a diet soda in front of me. Mark said, "Hold your left arm out to your side and hold that diet soda in your right hand." He was using the method called kinesiology or muscle testing that David Hawkins describes in *Power vs. Force: The hidden determinants of human behavior.*[2]

So I did and he said, "Now I'm going to push down on your arm and I want you to resist." He did and my arm was weak.

He said, "Okay, now bless the soda."

I said, "What do you mean?" I was kind of embarrassed; I didn't pray in front of anyone; heck, I didn't even pray alone at that point.

He said, "Just say something like, 'Bless this soda and make it healthy for my physical body and my spirit.'" I did as he suggested and he pressed down on my arm again and it was strong! It was so powerful for me. I immediately thought, "This is just great, because now I can just bless all the crap that I eat and it will be healthy for my physical body and my spirit! What a concept!"

So there really was something to the religious concept of blessing the food that we eat. I tried to get into the habit of blessing my food and drink all the time because, as I could see with kinesiology, it is so simple and so effective.

If you can bless a diet soda and change its impact on your body, just think what you might do if you carried the idea forward to another person or even yourself!

Dr. Masaru Emoto's book, *The Hidden Messages in Water*[3], supports this concept of being able to bless something or think positively about something and being able to change it. You can actually physically change it. He talks about showing love and compassion to water and showing hate to water and even just putting those words on a water bottle and being able to alter the crystalline structure that is formed by the partially frozen water. There are many amazing photographs to prove it. The book supports the concept of being able to alter things around you with your thoughts.

Help Yourself

I originally met Debbie after she was in a car accident that caused severe memory impairment. I never directly treated her, but I knew who she was. So I recognized her when she showed up at my yoga class. She never remembered my name, but she always knew who I was.

Debbie started coming to yoga at a time when something started shifting for Julie. The veil that blinds us all from seeing Spirit clearly, was already very thin at that time for her. She could already communicate with Spirit on a verbal and auditory level. She could also see spirits and ghosts. What seemed to be a primary change was that now she could *always* see the spirits that are around us, healing and guiding us.

We were in our down dog position, heads upside down, and I could see Julie's black ponytail bobbing as if she was looking around the room. I caught her attention and flashed her a quizzical look. She opened her eyes really wide back at me, signaling, "You have got to see what's going on here!" I had a tough time waiting through my sun salutations, warrior poses and cool-down stretches.

As the class cleared out, I said, "You have got to tell me what was going on. You were looking all over the place!"

She said she was seeing beings moving around the room and touching everyone—but they didn't touch Debbie. They looked like hooded monks. In her mind, she said to them, "You go back and heal Debbie, too."

Spirit said, "No, she's not asking."

Julie said, "I don't care that she's not asking, you go back and heal Debbie, too." She was always very commanding with Spirit and never just accepted everything it said. Spirit reiterated that nothing could be done because Debbie wasn't asking.

Julie said to me, "You've got to talk to Debbie and you've got to get her to ask for help or she won't make further progress." I didn't understand because Debbie was a very religious, very spiritual person. We had had talks about her disabled grandson and her daughter and she knew that it was all happening for a reason, and that God had saved her from her car accident for a reason. She talked about praying to God every night for her children. So I didn't understand. I thought she had all her beliefs in place.

I didn't know how to have the conversation without revealing all the details. But Spirit helped. The next time Debbie came to yoga, I said, "Debbie, we've had a number of talks about spirituality and about God's role in your family." She nodded in agreement. "Do you ever pray?"

She said, "Oh, yes, every day!"

I said, "Do you ever pray for yourself?"

She immediately replied, "No! I pray for my daughter and my grandson. If God is going to help anybody, then I want Him to help them first. I've lived a very good life and I don't need Him to help me."

I chuckled at this and said, "Debbie, you're only fifty-two years old! You've got a whole life ahead of you."

She said, "Oh, no, I want Him to help my daughter and my grandson."

I responded, "If you had three children, would you want God to help only two of them?"

She answered, "No, I'd want Him to help every one of them."

I said, "Don't you think God wants to help all of His children?"

She looked at me like I had just said something important and I hoped with all my heart that I had! She replied, "But I want Him to help my daughter and my grandson."

"Do you think His resources are limited?"

"No."

"Then, Debbie," I urged, "you need to pray for you, too. I'm going to pray for you as well."

She said she would pray.

The next time I saw Debbie, I hoped that some little window had opened so that Spirit could get in. That was all Spirit needed. I knew there was a likelihood that she would not actively be praying for herself because she would forget, but I also knew that Spirit probably just needed that door open and would understand that she was open, even though she could not remember on a conscious level. When I met up with Julie at the end of class, she had a huge smile on her face and she said, "Spirit went over and touched Debbie!"

Debbie began excitedly telling me over the next few weeks, how her memory was improving. It also coincided with a medication change. Of course it did. There always seems to be a concrete reason that you can choose to believe as well. I believe that Debbie being touched by Spirit allowed the medication change to occur and that she received a spiritual healing as well. I choose to believe the spiritual reasons, while recognizing that the concrete plays a role as well.

Debbie's story continues to have tremendous impact for me because it showed me that "Ask and ye shall receive"[1] is completely true. I think it would be clearer, though, if it had been written, "You *have* to ask or you will *not* receive." I now ask for help from Spirit with everything and I remind Spirit regularly that I am always open to help, just in case I forget to ask!

Remember that Debbie was a strong believer, but she needed to specifically ask for help for herself. I would wager that many people think and pray in the same way as Debbie. They pray for other people, but don't ask for help for themselves.

Deadly Beliefs

I believe it is wise to ask for help from Spirit early and often. I have a theory that it is easier to get rid of a physical ailment before you even know it's there and what it is. Clearly, God can get rid of anything at anytime, but if you don't know it's there, then He doesn't need to deal also with you and your beliefs about how deadly it is, or how hard it is to get rid of, or how painful it is.

Consider, for example, the case of my mom's orange tabby, Rafferty. Rafferty's behavior changed drastically. This once loving cat would actually run at my mom and attack her. My parents took him to a trusted veterinarian who diagnosed Rafferty with a brain tumor. My mom and dad were devastated and scheduled an appointment with a specialist to determine treatment options.

I went over to their house to comfort them and spend some time with Rafferty. He let me put my hand on his head, so I gave him Reiki energy for a while. In typical cat form, he told me when he was done by abruptly getting up and walking away. My mom called me, ecstatic, after the appointment with the specialist, to tell me that Rafferty's brain tumor was only an infection and, after a course of antibiotics, he'd be fine. Of course, no one told Raff that he had a possibly deadly, incurable brain tumor, so changing it to something else through Reiki and prayer was no big deal.

We Need All the Help We Can Get!

Remember the story I shared earlier, when Julie became overwhelmed with all that Spirit showed her that she needed to do? When she doubted her ability to do all Spirit asked, it laughed and said, "You have never done things completely on your own. What makes you think you would do them alone now?"

It was humbling to be reminded how much we need Spirit working in our lives. It was also empowering to think about how much more we might achieve if we constantly asked for Spirit's assistance.

This story and Debbie's highlight the power that we do have to ask Spirit to be present and assist us. A recent experience solidified this idea for me. Julie and I were sitting together over coffee, and I was telling her about having listened to Meg Blackburn-Losey speak on www.worldpuja.org[5] about how we have the power to "command" Spirit to appear and give knowledge.

Just then I began to feel a tingle of energy at my throat, and Julie giggled. She said that a Spirit had been standing in the corner and when I began talking about commanding Spirit to appear, he came forward and touched me. I felt that touch. For people who cannot yet feel Spirit, just know and have faith that Spirit will come close when you call and will assist you.

Blackburn-Losey's use of the word command was a little uncomfortable for me because of the authoritarian images it brings up. However, it did get me thinking about the fact that we don't have to *beg* for help from Spirit, which some prayer traditions imply.

Most people just let events happen to them. They don't put themselves in the driver's seat, much less the Captain's seat. But all those Spirits are out there, *wanting* to help us—but they can't, unless they are invited or requested to do so. We are potentially powerful beings. We just have to step into our own power. Once we decide we want to do something or are guided to do something, then we *should* step into our power, like the Captain of a ship, and command the crew accordingly, while expressing our gratitude for the assistance.

A story related to Debbie's story involved Julie and a Jewish patient. Julie was making the rounds, visiting her cancer patients at the hospital. She had been calling on Jesus when she visited their rooms. This was a practice that she began when Jesus appeared to her in a meditation, and then began appearing regularly to provide guidance. This patient had not shown any noticeable change.

"Jesus seemed frustrated," she told me. "Jesus had been trying to help the man, but the man rejected Jesus and would not accept help. He said that I would have to work with Moses, because the man believed in Moses." Sure enough, Moses appeared the next time she went to the man's room and everyone noticed a change in the man afterwards. Julie told me that working with Moses had been a very powerful experience.

So we began to understand that we had to consider the person's belief system. If we called upon a particular Spirit to help, it had to be a Spirit that person could believe in, or accept help from. Jesus' frustration showed us that we are not the only ones who feel frustrated when a person will not accept our help. Spirit is behind us, wanting it just as much as we do.

Do Your Part

There's a joke where the man is sitting on his roof while everything is flooding around him. He prays to God to save him.

The Emergency Medical Service rows up on a boat and offers to save him. He says, "No, God will save me."

As the water continues to rise, a policeman rows by in a boat and tells him to jump in. The man says, "No, God will save me."

Then a helicopter shows up and they drop him a rope, but the man tells them the same thing.

So the man drowns and when he gets to heaven he asks God, "Why didn't You save me?"

God says, "What, the EMS, policeman and firemen I sent weren't good enough for you?"

Asking and then getting out of the way to let Spirit work are extremely important, but you must also know what *you* can do.

When Julie rented an office in November, she needed to renovate it, but she also needed to open it for business so she could start generating money to pay the rent. She was told by Spirit not to worry, that it would open by December first.

When December first came and went, she asked Spirit what was going on? Spirit said she was dragging her feet about scheduling workers and picking up materials, and she needed to do those things before the office could open. She did her part and the office opened a couple days later.

There Are No Accidents

Everything happens on purpose. Everything in your life has prepared you for where you are now. You chose things to happen in a certain way. The more you open yourself and allow things to happen as divinely scripted, the natural flow can occur and circumstances can be brought to you more quickly.

This is not to say, though, that our contracts are carved in stone. We do have lee-way and free will. And sometimes plans shift in a new direction. This may be why we see someone who appears to be completely on purpose in their life, but then changes to something else. It could be they had completed what they set out to do, or it could be that the contract changed to better utilize and reflect who they had become and what the world needed.

Be open; allow for possibilities other than the concrete. Listen for guidance. Keep your thoughts positive and reflective of your highest desires. Know that prayers and blessings carry energy and are powerful. Ask for assistance; don't go it alone. Step up and do your part, complete your responsibilities. Know that it is all with purpose.

Chapter 4
Speak the Truth

What's Your Truth?

Speaking your truth is another effective way to clear your channel and to step into your power as an energetic being. In essence, it is being true to your ideals through your words. The concept of "speaking the truth" was one of the first clear messages that I received during meditation.

I had been feeling a distinct vibration in my lips. At that time I was not feeling much vibration, so it was noteworthy. I understood that it meant that I was to speak, so I asked, "What am I to speak about?" Then I understood: "The truth." I didn't *hear* it, I *knew* it. It was an instance of claircognizance, or clear knowing.

I was so excited that I had actually gotten a clear message! I met Julie the next day and she said that every time I said "speak the truth," a bright glitter of energy shot off to the side in my aura.

I tended to be very quiet about my beliefs in spiritual matters. Anything else, and I would be sure to give you an opinion! But on spiritual beliefs, I would say little. I know that people who share their religious or spiritual beliefs are not always regarded seriously. They become categorized as "one of those," or as being too zealous, and they are often looked down upon. I know that when people used to talk to me about spiritual or religious things, I didn't appreciate it. I especially didn't think you should talk about those things at work.

But I began to feel that in order to be true to myself, I needed to include some aspects of my spirituality. I felt that I was holding back on potentially valuable concepts for other people. Sharing these ideas has the capacity to awaken people and there is no greater gift. Not that I wanted to go around preaching—that is not me at all. I just started to share little pieces of what I believed. Sometimes it was just a little phrase. Rather than say "good luck," I might say, "Believe you can do it." Or if someone was sick, I'd ask for the name of the person and offer to pray or send energy.

Out of My Comfort Zone

Occasionally I would find myself talking to someone about an aspect of spirituality that I hadn't intended to speak about. It would be so far beyond my comfort zone that I would say to myself with dread, "Oh, no! What are you doing? You've blown it big time." Yet in every one of those instances, I got tremendous positive responses and it seemed to be exactly what they needed to hear.

During healing sessions, speaking the truth means being guided to put something into words that is *their* truth. To say something that *they* needed to hear—something that was truth *for them*. Often I'm quiet during a session, but sometimes I'll feel an impulse to talk about something that I wasn't even aware was an issue for them, and it will touch them. I surprise myself and it isn't until afterward that I realize I was guided.

An opportunity for speaking the truth in a healing session came when a head injury client named Elizabeth came into treatment feeling very upset. Her team felt that she could benefit from the relaxation that Reiki often provides, so I was allowed to offer it to her during a free period.

I was nervous about approaching her with this offer. I was stumbling over my words and wondering how to describe it. Finally, I bumbled it out and she got a huge smile on her face, as she said, "I have Reiki Level 1 training and I would love that!"

What a relief! After that, the words just flowed from my mouth. I asked her what the pain was there for—what was its message? She was able to give me a reason and we discussed it, as my questions and comments flowed. I thought again, "Oh, no, what are you saying?" But we had a wonderful conversation as I gave her Reiki.

At the end of the session, she told me that she had come into treatment that day not knowing why she should go on living. Now she had hope. She hadn't judged me as I feared. She just accepted. And I gained another huge lesson in not worrying about what others think, and just trusting the guidance as it comes. Elizabeth showed me that I had many more answers, and I could help people if only I would *start* talking!

Mistaken Motives

Sometimes I'm amazed by the words that come out of my own mouth. For example, my friend Don was in a terrible accident. As soon as he could have visitors, I went to see him. He told me what happened: "My truck slid on black ice and flipped over in a ditch on the side of the road. I was there, unconscious, with a broken neck, for hours until an old man found me. I am so lucky that I survived that car accident and I know God was watching out for me."

I felt the impulse to tell Don the story about a visiting pastor who came to my church. He told us about being in a terrible car accident and then being in pain for many years. One day he went into an empty church and began yelling at God, "Why did you do this to me?" Then he heard a voice saying, "I didn't do this to you; I saved your life." Then the pastor realized that *he* was the one who had had gotten himself into a dangerous situation, but God saved his life.

Listening to the pastor, I realized that God did the same for me. It was a miracle that I survived my car accident years earlier. But He had helped me to use those circumstances to shape the most wonderful life that I'm living now. I was humbled that God had helped me, ashamed for having blamed Him for so long, and so very thankful for His assistance. It changed my interpretation of my accident from one of being a victim, neglected and alone, to being divinely rescued.

My story about the pastor seemed to have a similar effect on Don. He was sitting there with his jaw dropped open in amazement. I knew that he was reframing his thinking about his accident in his head. I gave him some time to do this and then I felt a gentle nudge and heard myself say, "And in your case, He probably said, 'Let me flip his truck over, because he's going to break his neck, and he won't be found for hours. He'll need to be upside down to provide traction on his neck so he won't become paralyzed.'" At this point, I sat with *my* mouth open, recognizing the truth in the words that had just come out of my mouth.

Follow the Nudge

Opportunities for sharing guidance are often presented to us. At the dentist one day, I felt guided to push a conversation with Jenna, the hygienist, further than I typically would. As I slid into the chair, she asked me the perfunctory question of what had happened since she had seen me six months ago. I told her that my father just had open-heart surgery. She said that her mother had open-heart surgery twice, but surprisingly, she said, heart problems were not what she died from. The topic was obviously still very hard for her to talk about, three years later.

Jenna said that sometimes she's able to talk about her mom without becoming emotional and that sometimes she begins to break down. She told me what happened to her mother, and then said that it was very hard not having a mother, and that she missed her very much.

My immediate thought was, "You do still have a mom!"

I was told, "Ask her if she ever feels her mom around her." That was too much for me. I hardly knew this woman! No way! She's cleaned my teeth once. That hardly makes it okay for me to have that level of discussion! I heard again, "Ask her if she ever feels her mom around her." Here we go again.

Jenna moved on to another subject before I could say anything, but the voice kept repeating in my head while I argued back and still tried to keep track of what Jenna was saying. I let her finish her new subject and then popped the question. "Are you ever aware of your mom's presence around you?"

She stopped dead and looked me square in the eyes as if wondering what I knew and who could have told me. I knew she was also weighing whether to tell me the next piece or not. She said, "No, I have not felt her around me, but I recently went to something called a Reiki session."

Bingo! I knew that, indeed, I was supposed to have this conversation.

I interrupted her awkwardness at this point to say that I was a Reiki Master Teacher. She was floored and the story flowed of her recent experience with a Reiki practitioner who had a clear connection with

Spirit. She told Jenna, who was divorced, that her heart had been numb for many years. Jenna knew this to be true. She also told Jenna that a "Margaret" was around her abdomen. She went on to describe Margaret and Jenna knew it was her deceased grandmother.

Jenna's grandmother wanted her to know that she approved of her current boyfriend. Jenna shared that she had been having dreams about being very happy with her boyfriend in her grandmother's house. She enjoyed these dreams, but was disappointed because she had not had another one since going to see the healer. I told her that the dream left because it was not needed anymore. The dream was only there to let her know that her grandmother approved of her relationship, and now the dream wasn't needed anymore.

We went on to discuss the nature of healing, dreams, energy and intuition. I think we both knew this conversation was special. I believe that we were there for each other that day. I needed to let Jenna know that her grandmother was with her, and that all of the things the Reiki practitioner said were true. I think our conversation helped her to open up to the possibility that there is a lot more going on out there than we can see. For me, Jenna gave me another confirmation that I can trust my intuition when it tells me to speak. In speaking the truth as I knew it, our conversation went so much further and was so much more meaningful than it ever would have been.

Sometimes Spirit puts us in the right place at the right time, to benefit someone else. I believe there are many times when we say something to someone that is deeply important for them, yet we are not aware that we did anything at all, and we don't realize how important our words were. Since we don't always have a clear sense of when we need to say something, it's important for us to speak each time we are guided to do so.

Tracy was just a casual friend until I had a sudden impulse to tell her about going to a healer/psychic and how amazing it was. Then Tracy looked at me so intensely that I thought, "Oh, no! What did I do?"

Actually, she was completely intrigued and was interested in speaking with him. That conversation carried our friendship to a much deeper level.

Tracy was much better at speaking her truth than I was. Even when she didn't have all the pieces, that didn't stop her. She would just go ahead and share her passion with other people. I thought I needed to have all the details figured out before I could speak. I soon realized I would never have all the pieces, and it didn't matter anyway, because I would be guided in what to say. Tracy was always well received, because people could feel her excitement, and they could hear the truth in her words. She was an inspiration to me.

Share Your Truth

By "speaking my truth," I don't mean quoting Scripture or anything like that (although it might mean that for you). I just mean talking about a book on a spiritual topic; sharing the latest synchronicity or Angel story that occurred in my life; or simply sharing my ideas of the world as I know it. I know this world to be an exciting place, where Angels abound, healings occur, energy flows, miracles happen, and people have so much more power than they ever imagined.

I need to be sharing things now. It is important to be planting seeds. As I speak, I keep in mind one of the things that was so remarkable about Jesus. He would speak just on the edge of what a person already believed. He would speak just outside that person's comfort zone. He would share that next piece. He didn't go too far beyond what they were able to hear.

Jesus is a model for me, in speaking with others about topics that may feel threatening to them. I try to speak at a place where they need to stretch conceptually beyond their current beliefs, but can still handle it without discounting it completely. I try to gently leave something out there for them to reach for, so they can take that next step, and find their own truth.

Don't Worry About Others' Opinions

It used to be very scary to me—this concept of speaking the truth. I felt like I would really be exposing myself to ridicule, or be regarded as less than professional among my peers.

Starting to write this book was a huge leap of faith, and a show of commitment on my part. Spirit urged me to write and I initially resisted because of my lack of experience. But I was learning to trust in Spirit and to know that they are privy to a bigger picture. My fear of what my family would think was a big part of the issue. This was a surprise to me.

Yet I reminded myself that we are here for a purpose. I absolutely believe we are. So many people are constantly searching to find this reason in their lives. Lack of finding it, I believe, contributes much of the depression that we have in the world right now. I know that I am here for a divine purpose, so it really doesn't matter what anybody thinks of what I do, because I'm living in my divine truth. If this is true, then on this side and on the Other Side, I will feel fulfilled, because I found my truth and I lived it.

So I began to have general discussions with family members, and I shared more of what was happening in my life and how my beliefs were changing. I also tried to share a little more of my experiences as they occurred, and my philosophy, so that they wouldn't be shocked when they read the book. I found several members of my family very receptive. In fact, my mother began sharing some of the odd things that she was experiencing. They listened to my stories, and we had some nice discussions. There didn't seem to be the judgment that I was worried about.

Imagine for a moment that you get to the Other Side. You realize that you were lucky enough to have found what your purpose was and you didn't do it because you were worried about what other people would think. How would you feel? You would be disappointed when you realized it was an opportunity to learn more lessons and to evolve spiritually, and you fell short of what was possible, because you worried about what others would think. Oh, and by the way, the "others" missed their lessons, too, because they were worried about what *you* would think!

I want to be doing what I decided to do before I incarnated this time around. I don't want it watered down by what other people will think. The opinions of other people shouldn't matter, as long as you're acting in integrity and aligning with your truth. Just go ahead and live in your truth, even if some people think you're "crazy." Be respectful of others' truth if it's different from yours. Be silent often enough so you can learn what your truth is.

As Andrea and I began to speak our truth more, it seemed that we were being guided to talk with people who would be more receptive. Or maybe people in general were more open to hearing about spirituality than we ever suspected.

Speak for the Benefit of Others

I was asked to do a presentation on spirituality and holistic practices in the treatment of people with brain injury. I was excited because of what it might do for the center. But Spirit told Julie that this speaking engagement was not primarily about what it could do at my work. It was, instead, to awaken others to the spiritual world around them. It's human nature to look at things from our own perspective, but sometimes our words and actions are there to assist others.

This guidance from Spirit reminded me how important our words and actions are in awakening others and humbled me to think of being used in this way. It made the presentation feel much more important. Afterward, we were told through guidance that the presentation had achieved its goals of awakening people, providing some healings, and helping me gain some comfort in speaking my truth publicly.

The Truth is Not Absolute

Keep in mind that the message is *speak* the truth as you know it; it isn't to *defend* the truth or *debate* the truth. Truth speaks for itself and defends itself. I fully understand if someone isn't ready to hear my truth. There's no need to attempt to convince anyone of anything. Having come from that concrete world, I know there was a time when nothing you could have done or said would have changed my beliefs. I needed to experience things for myself. I needed to have repeated experiences at a level that was so strong that I could no longer explain it away. Until that happened, mere words could not convince me.

On the other hand, once people have these experiences, they begin to seek the Truth, and they will be grateful when you share yours with them.

Of course, there isn't one absolute truth—at least, there doesn't seem to be. In each decade of my life, my beliefs varied, and in the last few years they have been changing even more rapidly. I keep being shown new things and understanding them in new and deeper ways. I believe that it's important to keep questioning *everything* I believe so I can be shown more.

We don't know all the answers, even when we think we do. We need to recognize this and be tolerant of everyone else's beliefs. It's much more fun and interesting for me now to listen and try to understand what someone believes and why, than it is for me to attempt to try to refute them and prove myself right. How do you prove faith and Angels and God anyway? Always respect that the other person's truth is right for them at that moment. Acknowledge their beliefs and allow them to live their lives as they choose. Nothing is broken, so there's nothing to fix. Be true to yourself, while respecting the truth of others.

In the end, be aware that you speak volumes just by the way you live your life. Teaching by example is one of the highest ways of sharing your truth.

Chapter 5
Awakenings

Everybody Up!

If you're being awakened repeatedly in the middle of the night, begin to question why. It may be for meditation; it may be for some other purpose. It might be that you should be writing, or painting or any number of things. You are being awakened in the night because your ego is the quietest then and you'll be more receptive to your higher guidance. I would advise you not to try to continue to sleep, because it probably won't work. Bite the bullet and get up, and you'll likely discover something beautiful.

As I said before, sometimes I'd wake up because I'd feel isolated vibrations in various places in my body. I was only able to feel them when I was very still. Eventually, I began to feel the energy build up in my body and it kept my body moving and awake. I didn't know that it was energy in the beginning; I just knew that I was physically uncomfortable. It took me a very long time and a lot of experience feeling energy before I realized that was what it was. I wasn't used to thinking of things in energetic terms.

I suspect that some people who experience Restless Leg Syndrome are simply experiencing the build-up of energy in their body. I had RLS symptoms for several years. It wasn't until I began doing Reiki and became better at moving energy through my body that these symptoms began to subside. It felt like there was too much energy stuck in my body, and I didn't know what to do with it.

Over time, I tried various things to release the energy. One thing that worked very well was Epsom salt baths. Some nights I realized that the "fidgets" weren't going away without a bath, so I'd get up at two in the morning and take a bath! This was so against my nature. In the past, I'd force myself to stay in bed until I fell asleep again. Now I was getting up to take baths and to meditate!

Good Vibrations

I now feel a lot of vibration in my body at night (and during the day, for that matter!). It feels good, but initially it was distracting because it was a new sensation. It started very small, just a little part of my body, but over time it grew to larger areas and then to my entire body. Over time, I became used to it. It feels wonderful and comforting. I could generally get back to sleep, but it was disturbing to my sleep, nonetheless. Often, if I didn't move, it would increase the feeling of electricity. I am not exactly sure what was going on during these times, but I believe that they were healings and signs that Spirit was close. As time went on, I'd open my eyes when I felt the vibration and I'd see a block or a swirl of color, which I learned was how an Angel or Spirit presents. Every Angel has a specific vibration that's associated with a specific color. Over time, by pairing the two, I was able to figure out who was with me. Now I ask for a specific presence to come in and I feel their familiar vibration and see their color.

There were also times when I'd feel like there was a ton of energy coming in that day, which would make it less likely that I would sleep well that night. I'd have to clear the energy first. I guess this is what some people call "grounding the energy." I just knew that it felt like I needed to get the excess out. It would take many instances of the same experience for me to realize that there was a pattern, and then to figure out what actually worked. I needed a guidebook!

Nighttime Healings

Sometimes I would be awakened for healings. A night or two after my father had his open-heart surgery, I was awakened. I thought I was supposed to meditate, so I sat and meditated and went back to sleep. Then I woke up a second time, and I was shown a cross. I understood that Jesus was present. But I wanted to go to sleep! I was so tired. Even though I knew that Jesus was there, I still wanted to go to sleep. Then I was shown that it was connected to my dad and I knew that Jesus was there to help heal my dad. How do you turn that down?! If Jesus was there to heal my dad, then I was in! I wanted to heal my dad, too. I called forth the presence of my father and did a distant healing session.

Most often, though, the healings seemed to be for me. Initially, they were the full-body vibrations I described above and they were typically unsolicited. I'd just lie there and begin to feel the vibration. Over time, the full-body vibrations would still happen, but I'd also feel specific parts of my body being worked on—often it was a specific chakra, but it might also be some painful area.

With more time, I would feel Spirit and I would know who it was. Archangel Michael has a strong vibration that I feel across my chest and upper back. Jesus has a subtler vibration that I feel in my arms and face. I feel Ariel as a blanket of warmth and energy across my neck. Gabriel and Raphael present as a full-body comforting vibration. Jophiel has a strong vibration that I feel in a concentrated area around my mouth.

Nighttime Travel

I learned through stories that Julie would tell that we all have the ability to go on night visits to other people. This is called astral travel. It happens all the time, but you don't always know it. According to Julie, she, Andrea and I would travel as a pack at night and go and heal or go and talk with someone. Perhaps we were supposed to awaken them spiritually, I'm not sure. I didn't remember traveling, but I trusted that it was happening.

Our spirits aren't stuck behind the veil like our conscious selves are. They know what they're capable of doing, and what they're here to do, and they go off and do it! The dense, physical body isn't always a fun place for your spirit to stay, even though it learns useful lessons through it. So it likes to leave at night when it can.

Another friend had been talking about a potential health issue. She was going to have it checked out by her doctor. Julie said that we had gone to her in the night to talk to her, because she was in the middle of choosing whether to be sick or to be well. We were going to her to attempt to convince her to be well. Another night she said we went to my friend

Don, who had flipped his truck over, to give him some energy because he was depleted and on the verge of having a heart attack.

Once I learned these night visits were possible, and happening anyway, I began to set my intentions during the day to visit someone that night. I'd trust that I was going in the nighttime to assist those people. Sometimes when I would create a particularly long list of people to assist, I'd realize that I had a restless sleep that night.

You don't have to wait until nighttime to send your energy or consciousness off to help someone else. I set my intention out loud to visit someone that night, while I was with Julie. She said, "Why wait until nighttime?" It certainly makes sense that we wouldn't need to wait. I guess I just assumed I could use all the help of my consciousness that I could get while I was awake! But she made me consider that might not be the case. So now I say that I would like to visit that person for healing, whenever it is in the highest good of all.

Give Me Strength

I used to be one of those people who required eight hours of sleep. I planned my life around it. Little did I know how much fun it was to get up at night. I often was tired the next day, but, typically, it wasn't as bad as I expected. I began asking Spirit to give me energy to stay awake the next day and do what I needed to do. It worked.

We received the message that if ever we were tired, we needed to operate more from the heart energy, as this would give us the energy we need to make it through the day. That worked, too. You know how you're more irritated when you haven't slept well and people get on your nerves? Send them love. It will absolutely change your interactions with them.

Numbers in the Night

For a couple of months before beginning this book, I periodically received number messages. For example, I frequently received the number thirty-nine which meant "Get to work, Lightworker,"[1] on your divine life mission. For a while, I didn't know what my mission was and I would get very frustrated.

I would say, "I would gladly get going on it if you would just tell me what it is!" These number messages began to pick up in earnest once I knew that I was supposed to write this book. It was just uncanny how every time I would wake up (or be woken up!) in the middle of the night, the time would have a nine at the end. All of the number messages with 9 at the end – 09, 19, 29, 39, 49, 59, 69, 79, 89, and 99 – relate to getting to work on your divine life mission. That meant I was supposed to be writing at these times, as opposed to meditating.

As with the night-time messages to meditate, I fought it for the first three nights, arguing that I was on a leave of absence from work and that I had time to write during the day. I understood, though, that when I returned to work I wouldn't have the time to write during the day. I also knew that I'd be much more receptive to Spirit's guidance if I wrote in the middle of the night. So I fought these messages for the first three nights, but I knew that ultimately I had no choice. Writing this book is something that I chose to do before I incarnated, and I didn't want to let *myself* down. By the fourth night I just got up.

Spirit had been waking me up in the middle of the night to meditate for several years, but then Spirit began giving me the "get to work" number at the same time, so I knew that I was to be writing and not meditating. In fact, during this time, I spontaneously began to sit and meditate just *before* sleep. Normally I would be reading before bed, but during the time I was writing I had very little desire to read, so I meditated instead. This was extremely convenient, because since I'm still in physical form I do still need some sleep! With a few exceptions, I was able to function pretty well during my days, and I adjusted to this big disruption. In fact, I began looking forward to my writing times, knowing that Spirit was very close and that I was living on purpose.

Messages in the Night

As time progressed, I found myself waking in the night with the answers to questions I had been wrestling with during the day. I was never aware of having a dream about the issue. It was as if someone tapped me on the shoulder to wake me, whispered the answer in my ear, then ran off before I could see who it was.

Sometimes the message was for me, and sometimes it was for someone else. One evening I was having a deep conversation with my friend, Donna. So many seemingly negative things were happening that appeared to be out of her control. She coped by turning to alcohol.

I told Donna that I had been shown the number 45 over and over again. I knew that four is for Angels and five is for change. I looked it up because those numbers kept appearing. Normally, I would have just taken it to mean, "the Angels are with you through this change," but since it kept appearing, I looked it up. It turns out that 45 means, "The angels ask you to make necessary life changes without delay. You already know what those changes are. Ask the angels to help you find the courage and strength to make them, and know that these changes ultimately benefit everyone."[2]

Damn. I knew what those changes were for me.

I knew I needed to eat better and take better care of my body. I had been struggling with these issues for years. Damn. I *love* food. If we're talking about living in your joy, food is one of my joys. But I had been putting my body aside for the last, oh, about fifteen years, to take care of those around me. My weekend yoga could hardly keep up with my sitting behind a desk all week and picking on any food that was convenient. The thought of cleaning up my act and undoing all the harm I had done to my body was daunting. I hoped that if I just kept quiet about it, the Angels would let me slide. No such luck.

I knew that making the changes *would* ultimately benefit everyone, because they would help me to become a clearer channel. Anytime *anyone* becomes a clearer channel it benefits everyone, because it brings more light and love through you into this world.

Damn.

It might not seem like that big a deal to you, especially if you are one of those enviable people who were born skinny and managed to stay that way your whole life. But I wasn't and I didn't. And did I mention I love food? Gooey food, sweet food, salty food. All food. Oh, the pressure! Now I was no longer needing to watch my food intake for myself. Now I had to watch it for the whole world. Yes, I took it that seriously.

"Get to work, Lightworker."

Damn.

When I told Frank about forty-five and its meaning, he immediately knew his issues as well. You probably know yours, too. You may as well get to work on them now, rather than wait for the Angels to remind you. Because, in some form or fashion, they will.

Anyway, I told Donna about the meaning of 45 and she was truly stumped. She knew, of course, that the alcohol needed to go, but she couldn't see the point in bothering to give it up because she couldn't see how being sober would solve any of her problems. We sat quietly, thinking about what else she could change, but couldn't think of anything that she hadn't tried before. It was sad. I couldn't give her any reason that she would accept to get off the alcohol.

That night I woke up with a message for Donna. The message was, "Why would I give you anything more to work on when number one (the alcoholism) is so big? You will get numbers two, three and four (the next issues to work on) when number one is taken care of."

That made perfectly good sense and I almost felt foolish (ok, I did feel foolish) for not seeing it myself. Donna would have to change her life before her life could change.

There was such a sense of love and compassion for Donna within that message. That's what really struck me. Spirit knew that overcoming the alcoholism was going to be a major task, and would take great strength and courage. I knew that Spirit would be there to support Donna if she asked for help.

This type of very clear message seems to come out of the blue, which helps me to recognize that it has come through the channel, as distinct from my mind or ego.

Embrace the Night

Begin to be attentive to the time you are waking up at night. Is it exactly the same time every night? Is there a message? Do you feel like you should be doing something (whether you know what it is or not)? Try to sit up and just be still. Do this consistently. Be patient. You may not feel anything for a while. But just trust.

Remind yourself that nighttime is no different than the day in the sense that you are safe and Spirit is always around anyway. Remind yourself that at night, Spirit can get through to you better. Sit up and allow Spirit to lead you to healings, to true awakenings and to your divine life mission.

You won't be disappointed.

Chapter 6

Operate from Love

Are You Feeling the Love?

The vibration of love is a high vibration. The easiest way to tell that something is a high vibration is when it feels good at every level of your being. Operating from a position of love is very healing. It helps you to clear your channel, and clearing your channel helps you to operate more consistently from love. Operating from love keeps you in that good vibration and exudes it to everyone you're dealing with. The more you can respond from a perspective of love, the more you'll be able to keep yourself out of the lower vibrations of anger, jealousy, fear, guilt and sadness.

Operating from love means being willing and able to see the other person as just another soul trying to negotiate their way through the world, and through their life lessons. You see the events being presented to you as gifts from which to learn.

Your perspective is changed when you operate from love. It means you always intend to respond in a loving, caring and respectful way toward everyone, and every situation. The truly amazing thing is that when I'm able to maintain my position of love, I don't get mad or angry or hurt. I just get it—the whole picture—and I love each player for playing their part.

Operating from a position of love takes time to develop. Think about how often you don't operate from a loving perspective. But it's always the right time to start trying. I'm not totally there yet, but I'm much further along than I used to be.

Seven Tools to Increase Your Ability to Operate from Love:
Here are seven tools that have helped me to attain and maintain a position of love.

1 – Meditate
Meditation can help you to enter into a place of calm, and lack of judgment. This feeling tends to grow over time, so it's an extremely good place to start.

The technique that works well for me is to sit comfortably with my legs crossed like a pretzel (in the old days we called it Indian style), with my spine straight and head level. I place my hands on my knees with palms up and one or two fingers touching my thumb. Sometimes I begin by breathing deeply, but I often fade into a more relaxed style as I go more deeply into meditation. I am aware of my thoughts, but I don't pursue them. Generally they fade.

There are many styles of meditation and many books and teachers. Use a method that will compensate for any specific difficulties you are having. For instance, use a walking meditation if you tend to become physically restless when you meditate, or use a guided meditation if your mind wanders.

2 – Breathe
Use your breath to pull in energy, and to keep a constant flow of energy around and within you. A restriction in flow equates with a restriction in love. So you want to breathe deeply, to keep the energy flowing. Chapter 12 on *Clearing Energy* gives some specific tools. It's important to use your breath daily in non-challenging situations, but it's even more important to use it in circumstances that might otherwise cause you to fall away from your center of love.

You know those times: you argue with your husband over a misunderstanding because you're stressed; you're supposed to drive your son to his soccer game and he's dragging his heels getting out the door; your daughter is yelling at you for no reason; and the puppy just peed on the rug. Breathe.

3 - Ask for Help

When you realize that you're so angry or stressed or freaked out that you simply cannot operate from love, just ask for assistance from Spirit. Don't rely solely on yourself. Ask Spirit to help. When I'm going through my own challenging times, and my reserves are low, I don't have the same patience for my family and friends and clients who tend to rely on me for support. I may be needing love and support myself, and I may not have enough to give. Or they may be indulging in a behavior that is challenging to me—like kids whining! That's when I ask for assistance from Spirit.

My cues for knowing when to ask are when I feel angry, depleted or irritated. During these times of feeling challenged by others, I ask for Spirit to fill me with love. That is literally what I say, "Fill me with love, fill me with love." I may say it over and over again in my head, to stop me from saying aloud what I *really* want to say! It helps me tremendously to not say something I will later regret, and to be able to hang in there for the other person, which is what I want to be able to do.

4 - Watch Your Thoughts

Watch every thought and ask yourself: Is it coming from a place of judgment? Is it coming from a place of anger? Or is it coming from a place of love? Look at what you're saying about people and situations. Then simply correct that thought. In my experience, it's not hard to find a way to change the thought. The challenge is to be continually monitoring what you're saying so that you notice when there is something that needs to change. We all fall into automatic patterns—most of which we learned from our parents—that we do not want to imitate. An example might be criticizing a family member, in your head or out loud, rather than praising what you love about them. Once we've spotted something that's not coming from a place of love—it's typically something harsh or judgmental—then we can change it.

5 - Seek Out Others

It's easier to operate from a position of love if you surround yourself with like-minded people. Some of your old friends may begin to fall away, like the one who tells you that all bosses are unfair. Instead, the ones who come from a place of love will encourage you to stay in a frame of reference that supports love. They may remind you that there are lots of stresses that go along with being a boss that we don't always think about.

On the other hand, when you are being continually abused by a boss or spouse, a friend may encourage you to remove yourself from a situation so you can be in the company of those who share your values.

The more you surround yourself with like-minded friends, the more you'll be able to stay in a position of love. Once you become stronger, then you can occasionally be around those who are not operating from love, and they may benefit tremendously from being around you.

I've been in numerous situations where people have been judging other people. I try not to get caught up in the gossip. Instead I'll say something like, "Really? That has not been my experience with her at all," or "It sounds like she's very angry—how can we help her?" This will often stop the judgments, or take the conversation down a more positive path.

I feel disappointed in myself when I do occasionally get caught up in talking negatively about someone, so I try to go back afterwards and say, "I'm sorry I said what I did about Janet; I think she must be really scared (or whatever fits the situation)."

When I can express my feelings this way, it reminds me that I wasn't operating from love and it indicates to the other person that this is not the kind of conversation I want to be having. It gives me a sense of neutralizing the words I said earlier. Being judgmental about someone lowers your own vibration and lets in more darkness, causing you to lose space for light.

The tendency to gossip can be a hard one to overcome. It was for me. When we don't know what to talk about, the easiest thing is to talk about someone else. If that happens, try to keep those conversations positive. Talk about what you appreciate about them and think about how you can best assist them.

6 – Send Love

Consciously send love to every situation. I try to connect to a position of love within myself and to consciously send it to a situation, especially if I'm feeling angry. I do this by inhaling deeply into my heart chakra, and then I imagine blowing that energy out through the center of my chest.

I try to stop, back up, and consciously send love to that situation and the people involved. It's hard to stay mad or defensive when you're operating from a position of love. When I'm feeling bored, sitting in a meeting, I entertain myself by sending love to the entire scene—people, plants, animals. Hey—there are worse ways to entertain yourself.

When my daughter was fearful about progressing to the next set of skills in gymnastics, Will told me to send her love. He said that attempting to reason her out of her fears wouldn't work and would only entrench her more firmly in her fears, creating conflict between us. That was exactly what had been happening in my efforts to help her. For the next meet, the two of us rode alone in the car on a four-hour trip to Connecticut. I spent the whole time chatting with her about light subjects and sending her love from my heart. She was giddy by the time we got there and had the meet of her career!

7 – Change Your Perspective

When you find yourself being negative, try changing your perspective. For example, when someone is doing something that annoys me, I tell myself, "It's just another soul doing the best they can. This person is operating from one space right now, but he or she can awaken and change at any time."

I try not to judge where that person is right now. I remind myself that there is a larger picture and that we are *all* just souls trying to figure out our lives. That can really change how you think and behave. It changes the need to be better than others. It gets easier and easier with time and practice.

Even in times of war, both sides believe they're right. Most people try to do what they believe is right. So I try to look at *why* they believe they are right. Even when someone is hurting another through their words or actions, they believe they're justified. I look for that perspective. That doesn't mean that I agree with their perspective. I try not to judge anything. I simply try to recognize that their perspective exists, and that's why they're operating the way they are. I try to *understand* their behavior so that I don't *react* to it.

It also helps me to remember that that person may be giving me an important gift for my soul's growth. It's not always easy to thank someone for providing you with an uncomfortable situation. They may have sabotaged your job; put you on the brink of financial ruin; stolen your wife; or a million other things that you don't feel like thanking them for. When you can pull back, it helps to see the situation for what it is—a lesson. That "awful" situation may be just what you needed to direct you on your path.

I'll be honest. I don't always get the concept of "we are all one." We all experience ourselves as separate people. But when we begin to operate from love, we remember that we have also made mistakes; we have acted selfishly; we have been obnoxious at times, too. When we can forgive ourselves, it makes it easier to forgive others, and this helps us to feel that we are truly all one. Changing my perspective in this way helps me to not get caught up in the drama of the situation, and to not get caught up in fueling the dramas of others.

For example, two of our friends are getting divorced and, as you might expect, there is a lot of anger. She wanted the split and he did not. I speak with her more. She brings different dramas to me to vent and I try hard not to fuel those dramas. I constantly show her his perspective and refuse to judge him.

So when he does something that she doesn't agree with, my response is, "Of course that's the way he would react; he's feeling betrayed by you. Isn't that the way you would react?"

I'm not trying to tell her he is right, and I'm very clear about that with her. She continues to listen to me and to seek out my opinion because, by not being fueled, it takes away some of the intensity of her anger, and she doesn't really *want* to be angry with him. She's capable of seeing the larger perspective. When she talks with me, it helps her to get over the feeling of being wronged or taken advantage of, and needing to hurt back. It changes her behavior, because she no longer feels a need to retaliate.

But beware, because many people do not want to hear the other person's perspective. They aren't willing to consider the other side of the story. They prefer to talk to people who sympathize with their plight, and echo their own perspective. They want to stay in the drama.

Our Biggest Challenges

Frank and the kids are my biggest challenges to staying in the love (and, to be fair, I'm one of their biggest challenges!). It's ironic, because the relationships with the most love are also the ones that can make you feel the most anger. You don't feel anger if you don't care.

In arguments with Frank, Spirit helps me to change my perspective. When I can come from a position of love, and being able to consider his side, we have fewer arguments. But we still have them.

I remember the first time I sought Spirit's help in an argument with Frank. I was able, somehow, to stop myself from cursing at him in my head and ask Spirit to help me get through this situation. I was so intensely angry with him. I yelled in my head, "Tell me what to do! Tell me what to do!" But I really wanted Spirit to tell me how to win.

A quiet voice said back to me, "Love him anyway."

I argued with the voice, because its answer was not satisfying to me. I said, "No, really, I am so mad at him! Tell me what to do."

And I heard again, "Love him anyway."

"Love him anyway?!" What kind of answer is that? I didn't feel like "loving him anyway!" But the message was: "No matter what he says or does, love him anyway."

Over a series of successive arguments, it became a little easier, especially because the message from Spirit didn't change. Once you get to that place in an argument, the argument goes away. There's no need for it anymore. My first challenge was to *want* to drop the anger enough to find the love beneath it.

Using these tools helps to come from a position of love. I don't want to suggest that it's always easy, or that I always do it. It's my goal to be there, in the love, one hundred percent of the time.

Through multiple messages, it became clear that we are to operate from a position of love *especially* when we're tired, because it can help us overcome the fatigue. I guess that's what I experience when I feel challenged by the neediness of another person, and I feel like I have nothing left to give. I go to that position of love and find that reserve of strength and patience. Love is extremely powerful, and *you* are more powerful when you can operate from it.

Chapter 7

Fluctuations

Here We Go Again

You may think that once you embark on a spiritual life, things will be easy. They weren't for me, but they could have been easier if I had a broader understanding of what was going on. My hope is that having this information will smooth out your journey. While you are going through this process of awakening and spiritual evolution you may experience increased fluctuations in your emotions, and in the speed at which things happen. Issues that need to be healed may come up rapidly to be exposed.

Often the fluctuations in my emotions didn't seem related to anything in my life. Sometimes I was purging old things that needed to run through my body. In the beginning, after each Reiki attunement, I would experience a purging in the form of head-cold symptoms that would last for a week. With each attunement, the initiate experiences an opening in their energy body that allows more Reiki energy to flow through their body. Many Reiki students experience physical or emotional symptoms following their attunements, as the energy forces old issues to the surface. One of my friends cried for hours for no conscious reason.

During my spiritual opening, sometimes I experienced purgings unrelated to Reiki that probably had to do with being exposed to large amounts of energy. A couple times Andrea and I went through these openings together, and sometimes we could feel in advance that a purge was coming. We were told by Spirit that we would be lighter after these purgings, because something would be released. That was true.

Once I became very frustrated and angry with Spirit. I had just returned home from Sedona, Arizona. Sedona is a very high energy place, and I was probably overloaded. When I went home, I felt so sad. I was feeling so close yet so far. I longed for that conscious contact, like Julie and Will have. I was angry about needing to communicate with Spirit through others, instead of having my own direct connection.

I was mad because I knew that Spirit had the power to break through whatever block I had and I was upset with Spirit for not doing it. I was so mad that I said, "You may not talk to me now! Don't you dare talk to me!" I was throwing my version of a tantrum. "I am too mad to talk to you!"

When I finally spoke with Will Linville, he confirmed that there had been a lot of energy and information coming through in Sedona, and that we had contributed to the energetic grid of the Earth. The emotion I experienced was a shedding of old paradigms and energy patterns. It took a few days for the energy to work its way through and for me to feel like myself again.

It's always worth the emotional roller coaster, but my challenge, in the midst of the storm, is to remember that the upset is always tied to shedding or releasing something. That's a good thing.

I say to myself, "I choose to release this now so I can become a Clear Channel and further enhance my abilities to heal myself and others. As I release these old patterns, I am developing a clear connection to my guidance; I am living in alignment with my divine purpose, and I am in my full power."

Bad Times

In the old days, I would have described myself as being very even-keeled. But as I opened up, I experienced much more frustration, sadness and anger.

I made the decision to leave my job while I was on a family leave of absence. I realized that I had changed and that the job didn't make me completely happy anymore. I wanted to write and to pursue holistic healing modalities. The more I became clear that my purpose in life had shifted, the harder it was for me to stay. There was a vibrational discord.

Unfortunately, we were not quite financially ready for me to leave, so I ended up going through a period of sadness. Part of it was sadness over leaving the people and job that had meant so much to me, and part was sadness over not being able to leave right away. One of my lessons was to be okay in any situation. But I was not okay. I was having a hard time. I could get to a good place for a little while, but I had a hard time maintaining it.

I was making things harder for myself by not just allowing it to be, but I felt powerless to stop my feelings. I felt like a fraud, because I was almost done with this book and I thought I needed to be some kind of expert who could handle all of this better. Then Julie reframed things for me. She said I didn't need to be an expert, and I should take that pressure off of myself. She said to think of all of us (humanity) as being on a train, but in different cars. I might be in a car ahead of some others, but others were ahead of me, and we were headed in the same direction.

I'd still experience the same bumps and turns, but I could use my experience to warn others about what was coming, and I could report back on any hints or tips I learned as I traveled. That perspective helped a lot.

We all have bad days. When Frank mentioned to Will that he was having a bad day, Will responded, "By all means, my friend, have your best bad day ever." I think he was reminding Frank to enjoy the bad times, too. Yes, *enjoy* them. Experience them, live in them; don't try to escape. Live in the moment. This is your life.

I've gotten much better at living in the now and waiting to see where things go. In the past, I spent too much time aiming for a deadline, or a goal, or waiting for some fun future event. As soon as the special event arrived, I was already aiming for the next one.

Now I know: *Don't waste the time in between.* Experience it. Live it. You came here to experience *all* that this physical body has to offer. Don't miss it.

You will likely experience an intensifying of *all* your emotions. Just sit back and enjoy the ride.

Choices

A few months after I left work, I was having a discussion with Frank and Julie about how I could have better handled the sadness. Julie said that we can choose whether to be sad or angry in any given instant. I fought this vehemently because there were times that I absolutely did not have any control. The sadness was simply there and it was overwhelming.

As I stepped away from the conversation, I realized there was a lot of truth to the idea that we choose to be mad or sad. I could point to many instances where I had chosen to reframe things by looking at them from another perspective and thereby changed my emotional reaction. I was doing this more and more frequently. I also knew there were other times when I chose to allow myself to feel angry or sad.

But there were times when the sadness was so overwhelming I felt powerless to control it. When I felt angry, I practiced operating from love, and that helped tremendously. There was someone to direct the love toward. Sadness felt more inward. Perhaps the answer with sadness is to direct the love inward, toward oneself.

In any event, I believe that Julie is right. When we are angry or sad, we have chosen it. Emotions are part of our machinery, as humans. Emotions run through us like water. We shouldn't try to run away from our feelings. It's best if we can accept them, express them (hopefully in some harmless way), and then let them go. They only stay if they are fed by negative thoughts. That is where our choice comes in—we can choose to poke the bruise, or we can choose to move on. Consistently choosing not to harbor anger or sadness appears to take time for most people. The important thing is to be aware that you have a choice and to start trying.

Get It Yourself

Be patient with yourself when it comes to developing your true abilities. Remember, it takes time to clear your channel and that is part of the process. Attempting to speed the process will likely produce more fluctuations. I was not very patient in the beginning. Not at all.

Julie initially gave us a lot of guidance about ourselves and the process we were going through. Then Spirit started telling Julie that I could get the information on my own. I believed Spirit, so I went off and tried to get it on my own. Then I became mad, frustrated and sad when I couldn't get the answers I was looking for. I felt like I was being teased and taunted when the information didn't come. I didn't realize that Spirit meant a very different timeline. I thought Spirit meant I could do it right now, but no—I think Spirit was saying that I had the ability to go and get this wisdom or begin this process of receiving guidance. This was very different than what I had been looking for.

At one point, I needed a way to get rid of the pain in my knees. I was extremely frustrated because I hoped to relieve my pain immediately. Instead, it lasted for weeks, while I tried everything I could think of. In retrospect, I understand now that they were forcing me to become even quieter so I could develop my own guidance.

Eventually I was receiving my own guidance more clearly and more regularly. The frustration lifted because I didn't need Julie as much anymore. Some of the fun was gone, though, because I received a lot less detail. I might just have the knowledge that there was a change coming, for example, but she would know what the change was and why it was happening.

Over time, however, by listening, following my feelings and relying on myself, I began to receive more and more information on my own. Although I allowed myself to get very frustrated during that period in my spiritual growth, I realize now that it was incredibly important. It forced me to rely on myself and really begin to understand what was coming from my mind and what was coming from my intuitive inner voice or from Spirit.

Getting to each new step might not be easy, but it will come if you stay with it.

The Reason We Go Slowly

Julie, too, became frustrated at one point, because our tools were not coming fast enough. The Bible talks about a woman who just touched the hem of Jesus' garment and she was healed.[1] We were both asking for "hem of the garment" healing ability. We were frustrated because we were treating people and feeling their pain, yet we could not do all we wanted to for them.

One night, Julie was given a tremendous blast of energy and she became frightened. She thought she might be having a stroke or heart attack. She asked her guides if she needed to get help. They told her no, that she was fine. They wanted to show her that if they gave us too much energy at once (enough, say, to produce hem of the garment abilities), it would overload our systems, and our physical bodies couldn't handle it. To flow effectively and efficiently, the energy needs a fairly Clear Channel. If there is a block in the emotional or energetic bodies (the chakras) in the form of an unexpressed and unresolved emotional hurt or a dysfunctional belief system, then the energy will be impeded in its flow and pain will result.

So it needs to be a gradual process. We could get a bigger boost at one time, but we could not receive all of it at once. It reminded me that I'm always asking for more, more, more, but when I began to feel physically or emotionally depleted, I would lament about how hard this process is. I wanted to have my cake and eat it, too. I would get more of a boost at times, but then I would pay the price, either in my physical body or in my emotions.

I started to come to terms with the idea that I needed simply to ask for things to move as fast as I could physically and emotionally handle. I didn't want to be in physical pain and I didn't want to have too many emotional ups-and-downs.

Be patient with the perceived slowness. I hear many, many people committed to evolving who are dissatisfied with the slowness of the journey.

First of all, it's not going slowly. Get yourself a notebook and start journaling. Write down everything that happens—every healing, every intuition—everything. Look back in three months and six months and you'll see how much has changed. Don't be so hard on yourself—give it to God and trust that it is unfolding beautifully.

I am constantly reminded that things are so much more complex than we can comprehend; there is so much more happening behind the scenes than we will ever know. Even when things appear to be happening slowly, there are healings taking place and alignments happening. All of it is necessary before we can be where we want to be. Remember that it *must* happen slowly, or your physical body couldn't handle it. You'd be in pain and your emotions would be out of control. Recognize that the roller coaster *is* the change you're looking for. Enjoy the ride.

Wind-Up Airplanes

I began to realize that things seemed to be happening in waves. At one time, it seemed like there was a lot happening, a lot of revelations, an exciting healing, a new ability, etc. Then there would seem to be nothing for a while.

I received confirmation that that was indeed the way things were moving. It was like those old wind-up airplanes. It took time for it to get wound, and then the energy was released very fast, and the propeller turned very quickly. Then it would take time for the energy to build back up again as the propeller and its rubber band were turned again. This was how it felt for us. The energy needed to build so that it could be released and something could be revealed or an ability could be developed. Then there would *appear* to be nothing again for a while, as the energy built up.

Think about how many times you've met someone and thought nothing of it. Then, somewhere down the line you realize that this is the exact person you need to assist you in some way. Or you get a coupon in the mail for twenty percent off plumbing and two days later the sink breaks. The list of seeming coincidences is endless.

I was putting the pages of an ebook into a binder. I saw the top line of every few pages as I gathered and hole-punched them. One of them caught my attention because it said to remember that it takes time after you sow before you can reap. I was reminded to wait because it takes time for things to align. You don't pray and then immediately have what you prayed for. Sometimes it does work that way, but sometimes you have to wait for things to unfold. If you look closely, you can often see an amazing series of events that had to occur for your prayer to come to life. Things happen when the time is right. They won't happen before that. Sometimes that means waiting until you are ready—until you are *really* ready, not just when you *think* you are ready. Sometimes you have to wait until someone else is ready.

I know that I won't see Spirit fully until I stop being afraid to see them. I currently see colors, a vague shape or movement, and I have faith that the image will turn into something more definite as time goes on.

I sat in meditation one night, after months of saying, "Show yourself to me." I had my eyes open and the room was dark except for light coming in at the doorway. Then I felt my pupils starting to dilate and contract, as if they were trying to adjust to the lack of light. It looked like the door was opening and closing, and I became scared and then I knew I truly was not ready. Spirit would appear when the time was right. Things would have to change in me first.

Months later, as I was being awakened to work on this book, the door to the adjoining sitting room was blown open. As I mentioned before, that happened several times. But this time I sat up calmly and said, giggling a little, "Okay, I get it! You want me to get up and write now!"

I got up and went into the room to write and I realized that I had come a long way. In the past, if I knew that Spirit opened the door, I would have been terrified. Now here I was, about to walk into that dark room all by myself, and I was not afraid. Now I was giggling. I have made a lot of progress, and each day I'm closer to the kind of conscious contact with Spirit that I desire.

Fluctuations in Accuracy

Our little group experienced fluctuations in the accuracy of the messages we received. This was especially true for Andrea, because she tended to over-trust what she received, so she actually said it out loud, while I tended to under-trust it. If I dared to say it aloud, I was pretty darn sure of it. You would see false positives in Andrea and false negatives in me.

Andrea would be excited about guidance and it would feel so clear and so right to her. Then either life would play out showing she was wrong, or she would later receive contradictory guidance. This was very frustrating for Andrea. At one point they told her that she was 70% accurate and 30% inaccurate.

I said, "Well, that's as good as being completely wrong, because you never know when you're in the 30%!" And it was true. Until your channel is clear, you cannot have direct and always-reliable access to Spirit. In the early phases, expect to spend time cleaning out old dysfunctional belief systems, ego interference and false inner voices. That takes time and patience.

Until you build a clear connection with Spirit, you're going to have some hits and some misses. This process makes for a very frustrating ride and makes you completely doubt yourself and doubt the guidance that you're receiving because you think, "Well, if that was wrong, who knows what else was wrong."

I tended not to put any weight behind messages that I received. I tended to think it was just me thinking, and not guidance coming from Spirit. However, I would get confirmation that it was, indeed, guidance when Andrea had the same thought, or when life played out that way, or when Julie confirmed it. So I tended to get frustrated about not getting messages, and Andrea tended to get frustrated about inaccurate messages.

Just keep playing with your guidance and asking for it to grow. Know that inaccuracies are part of the process and welcome them as normal.

It will all unfold as it should. Keeping a journal really helped me to find some perspective on all of this. You can't see all of the changes day-by-day, but if you're writing it down, you can look back and see where you were and more fully enjoy where you are.

Stupid Plan

Just to illustrate how frustrated and annoyed I often felt, let me tell you about the "Stupid Plan."

When Julie told me that she couldn't give me guidance from Spirit, she also told me that I wanted it that way. I protested, "I do not! I want you to tell me the answer!"

She insisted, "No, this was part of your pre-incarnation plan so that you'd learn to get the guidance yourself."

In my frustration, I said, "Well, that's a stupid plan!" And I believed that for a long time.

After writing this chapter, I had the following conversation with Spirit.

"Why would I make myself suffer through months of knee pain if Spirit could tell Julie in an instant how to heal it and then she could tell me?"

"So you'd learn to heal yourself."

"Stupid plan."

Why would I get someone else's energy stuck in my body and not know why?"

"So you'd learn about the tools you have to heal others."

"Stupid plan."

"Why would I cry for days or weeks, feeling intensely sad and not know why?"

"Because we were healing you when you couldn't heal yourself."

"Oh."

"Why would I wait until I was 38 to awaken, most of that time believing there was no God, and then have to work so hard to develop my abilities, if I have always been connected to Spirit in all my lifetimes?"

"So you could be an average person—an Everyman—and show people it could be done."

"Oh."

"Each of those 'stupid' experiences will eventually be revealed to be lessons to help your soul evolve."

"Oh."

"You will realize that you learned more about God and life in those four short years than you had in your entire lifetime."

"Oh."

"You will realize you were being systematically taught the lessons of life so you could teach others."

"Oh."

"Maybe not so stupid?"

"Maybe not so stupid."

Chapter 8
Healing

You Are Perfect and Whole

So much of what will be happening as you open to evolving, clearing your body and raising your vibration can be called healing. You'll be healing thoughts, beliefs, behaviors, physical ailments, emotional baggage and even unresolved issues from other lifetimes. You may consciously choose to help others heal as well. In fact, just being in your higher vibrational presence will help them to heal, and will serve as a catalyst to their evolution.

Continue to Watch Your Thoughts

Positive thinking is important when it comes to health and healing. It's essential to disconnect from the collective consciousness so that you don't hold onto negative beliefs about aging, or what you might catch from being in a crowd, etc. Disconnecting from the collective consciousness is thinking fully for yourself. Examine your family's belief systems regarding aging, disease and healing. Consciously choose to keep the beliefs that serve you and discard or modify the rest.

For example, a man who constantly thinks, "I'm going to die young from a heart attack because that has been the fate of all the men in my family," may feel defeated and not attempt to take care of himself. On the other hand, he could reframe his family history by saying, "I'm going to eat well and maintain an active lifestyle so that I live a long and healthy life." The simple change in the statement of the belief system now invites health and rejects a negative outcome.

Your way of thinking is also important in specific instances of discomfort. When I have a recurrence of the pain in my knees, I simply acknowledge it and say, "Thank you for releasing that. I didn't realize there was still something there that I needed to let go of." I treat it as something positive, natural and needed. Often that's exactly what's happening and you don't want to trap it in your body by having a negative reaction to the sensation, by tensing up and holding onto it. Let it go! Visualize it releasing and imagine how good it will feel.

Identify the Message

Ailments that need healing are really messages from your body, whether they come in the form of depression, Restless Leg Syndrome, a headache or some other physical pain. Look beyond the overt symptom for the larger message behind it. Where is it coming from?

For example, think of a time when you cried. Where did you feel it in your body? When I cry, my shoulders and arms get tight and begin to hurt. It appears that my arms are the problem, but it's really the underlying emotion that's causing the physical pain. Dig beyond the physical symptom to identify the true problem.

A woman came to my office with what she perceived as a "deep, dark secret" that was "eating her up." She was thinking about sharing it with her counselor, but she was afraid of being judged. I said, "Think about your secret."

"Okay," she said and sat quietly thinking about it.

I said, "Now where do you feel the secret in your body?" She immediately grabbed her chest and said, "Right here!"

I said, "Look at what your secret is doing. You've just taken something emotional and allowed it to affect your physical body. You *must* tell the counselor and get it out of there!"

She immediately asked if she could tell *me* the secret. I said she could, and when she was done she said, "Oh my God! I feel better already!"

She subsequently told her counselor and thanked me the next day for encouraging her to let it out. Honestly, the secret wasn't bad, but we eat ourselves up with worry, guilt, shame and anger. So, consider where you hold your secrets. Where do you hold your embarrassment and guilt? What hurts when you're angry or stressed? Think about it. Then let it go. Sharing your story with someone else is often a good place to start. Holding it in doesn't serve you, and will only make you ill.

Remember Debbie, who only asked for God to help her daughter and grandson? Don't wait until you're ill or have a disease before asking for help. Ask when you are well. Ask to be shown behaviors and emotions that don't serve you, and ask for help in changing them *before* you become ill. Ask for assistance from Spirit and also ask for assistance from your friends, your family and others you trust. Ask them to pray for you, too.

Listen carefully to your body, your thoughts and your emotions. When something like depression or body aches, arthritis, ulcers, or the myriad of other potential challenges appears, ask "What's it here for?"

Go into quiet meditation, put your attention on the area where the problem is, and ask questions like, "What are you here to show me?" "Why are you here?" "How can I relieve this?"

Pay attention to the first thing that comes into your head. Don't allow your mind to censor or second-guess the answer. If you have difficulty, ask your conscious mind to step aside and ask your intuitive mind to take full control. I recently asked Spirit during a massage, "What is being released now?" The answer was "Old patterns." My conscious mind expected the answer to be stress. If you are confused about whether the answer came from your own thoughts and not from Spirit, don't worry. Just accept the answer and even write it down and then wait and see if it seems to be correct.

If you don't hear an answer immediately, don't worry. Some revelations will be instantaneous and some will come slowly, but they will come.

Be sure to consider all venues for healing, and pursue what is safest for your body. For instance, it may be prudent to seek medical advice and follow the prescribed recommendations, such as anti-depressants, antibiotics, insulin, etc. Don't be a spiritual martyr. You can continue your self-analysis and try spiritual solutions at the same time that you are following medical advice. Don't prolong getting appropriate treatment in the name of spirituality and don't suddenly go off medications without medical oversight.

There will be times when pain in a part of your body is simply energy that's stuck. Nothing is wrong, per se, but there's the potential for a problem to develop if the energy is not released. Try the energy-clearing techniques in Chapter 12: *Clearing Energy,* to help it pass. Remember to stay positive and do not identify the sensation as a problem.

When energy is releasing from my body, it is often accompanied by a quick pain, a discomfort, or a muscle twitch. I initially felt these energy releases in only two places on my body—the fleshy part between my thumb and forefinger and the back of my upper arm. Spirit focused the releases on these two areas until I figured out what they were, then the feeling spread to other parts of my body. I gained some insight about this by watching an acupuncturist give a demonstration. He put his needle between the thumb and forefinger and then he wiggled it and we saw a little spasm at the site. He said, "That's the chi (energy) being released." This was exactly where I felt my spasm. The releases felt like little muscle spasms without pain. It's like a tap, tap, tap from the inside.

If this happens to you, just relax and allow the energy to release.

Health Challenges as Lessons

My friend, Mark, was a jet-setting corporate executive until his higher self created a situation that produced a dramatic shift in his life. Mark was very satisfied, on one level, with his life. He saw the stress involved as a given and didn't realize what problems it could create for his body, mind and spirit.

After pushing himself hard for many years, Mark was diagnosed with cancer. We create dramas and traumatic situations in our lives to teach us lessons. A drastic situation might afford the best circumstances to learn a major lesson. It might be the only way a person would even recognize the need for a change. Mark changed his life completely, as he focused on holistic health, self-healing and helping others. Mark is now cancer-free.

Many people blame God for their illnesses. We need to realize that God did not "do this to us." We chose it. The soul made the decision, not the self, or the ego. You needed this event to happen for your own soul growth.

"Okay," you ask, "Then why did my husband (or my child, or mother, etc.) have to die? Surely no good can come from that."

Well, that death might make you stand up and become independent or take a risk. Sometimes it is about the other person's experience and what they came here to do. Not everything that touches you is about you, per se, although I do believe there will be opportunities to learn from almost everything.

Sometimes you are simply along for the ride, or to provide support for that person's journey. There could be many possible lessons and that doesn't mean that you won't be devastated by the loss. The soul or higher self takes the higher perspective. That's why I have, on typically sad occasions, said to my higher self, "I don't care what you say; this was a stupid plan! I hate it! If you think it was so smart and perfect, then you get down here this instant and experience this fully with me! Maybe that will teach you to make a better plan next time—one that won't hurt so much."

I really have done that. Yelling at my higher self helps the part of me that is entrenched in the dense, physical world feel a little better. The reality, though, is that my higher self was there the whole time, knowing the higher perspective, comforting me and cheering me on the whole way.

So look at the lessons that each circumstance affords you. You may need to change the way you think about something. You may need to change your behavior. You may change the way you look at the people in your life because you almost lost them. You may learn to slow down and appreciate things. You may recognize that the material things don't matter so much. You may realize that you have forgotten your divine life mission. You might even change the way you look at the person who is "victimizing" you, and thank that person (and consider leaving).

There are so many potential lessons. If we could change our perspective to look at life in this way, much would change about our lives. However, when people used to say to me, "This happened for a reason," it would irritate me. It was one of the worst things you could say to me.

How could my life be so disrupted; how could I be so depressed and in such incredible pain, with my ears ringing constantly—how could any good be connected to that? It was an insane concept. It seemed like a platitude that people said because they didn't know what else to say. Now I feel badly when I say it to other people, because I know how hollow it can sound. Sometimes it's simply best to let them figure it out on their own.

Yet I have seen one thing after another that the car accident brought to fruition in one way or another. Good things. Amazing things. Other seemingly negative events have also produced good changes. I still wouldn't choose to go through those circumstances again, but I can see that the changes were positive.

The soul wants to learn; the soul is here to learn. So anything that can teach the soul is a positive thing (at least from the soul's perspective). I do believe it's possible to learn the lessons without all the emotional upheaval. I think it's the resistance to change that causes some of the grief and the painful situations. I'm looking forward to learning lessons in the future without unnecessary pain! We need to consider that the pain (physical or otherwise) is the lesson. We try to avoid pain and all negative feelings without recognizing that, at times, painful lessons are the swiftest and most impactful. From the Buddhists comes the aphorism: "Pain is inevitable, suffering is optional." If you are alive, you can be guaranteed that you will feel some pain. No amount of spiritual growth can insulate pain from the human experience. The choice of what you do with the pain is your own.

Examples of Healing

I have witnessed many healings in myself and others. Personally, I no longer experience the neck, back, hip and shoulder pain that I had for over twenty years after the auto accident. I tried every way to directly attack the physical symptoms. I remember giving gratitude for the rare moments that I did not have pain. I never imagined that I could feel this good again. The pain slowly lifted as I slowly began to awaken. It went away as I healed the underlying problems.

Andrea experienced a healing of breast cancer; it was a good example of combining the spiritual and the medical. She did everything medically necessary, including having the lump removed. Spirit told Julie that I needed to allow Andrea to do Reiki on me, in order to heal *her*.

This request was confusing, because it seemed like it needed to be the other way around. But Spirit persisted and I relented. Partway through the session, I knew I needed to put my hand up and reflect the energy back to her. We both saw a zigzag pattern bounce from Andrea's chest to my hand and back again, so Andrea was getting back the energy she was sending out. Spirit used me to amplify the energy she was channeling and used it to heal her.

Sarah, my cousin, was given information that she needed to mourn her grandmother in order to reduce her immune system problems. As she began to let go of her grief, she developed a black line down her back. Oddly (or maybe not!) she began to feel much better and interpreted the black line as a healing, with the negative aspects passing out of her body. She chose to view it positively and it quickly went away and left her feeling better. Had it been accompanied by pain or discomfort, or had it persisted, she would have sought medical attention, but she was sure the black line was to show her concretely that a healing was occurring.

I have personally experienced or witnessed many amazing things during hands-on healing, including: knowing where a problem is; knowing what the problem is; what caused it; how to heal it and more. On a number of occasions I have felt something in a part of my body and known that I needed to move to the corresponding area on the person I was working on. I found a rash on the wrist of a woman who was paralyzed and mute from a condition that presented like ALS. I felt burning in my palm as it passed over her wrist which was covered by her sheets. In the same way, I knew on several occasions that she needed her airway to be suctioned. I had briefly felt short of breath and knew that her breathing was being impacted.

The first day I met my friend, Morgan, she knew which knee I had recently injured, because she heard crunching in her head when she touched that knee. Reiki practitioners often know exactly where to put their hands. A friend of mine, Lisa, had another Reiki-attuned friend walk up to her out of the blue and put her hand on the right side of her back above the waist and say, "How's your kidney?" Lisa's right kidney had just been diagnosed as having stones in it. Lisa was floored.

These things and much more happen daily in the lives of energy healers. There is nothing unique about these people. We all have the gift of healing but some have chosen to cultivate it. Spend some time talking to them and you'll be amazed by their stories. Then go do it yourself. You can, you know.

In fact, your body already knows what to do. Will Linville frequently reminded me how powerful our bodies are in their capacity for self-healing. He'd tell me that the body knows exactly what to do and it will go about healing itself if we let it. He'd tell me to say, "Body, take care of this." We block our body's capacity for healing by letting our minds get in the middle of things. It's a very simple first step in the healing process: Put the body back in charge.

Breaking Patterns

We need to be alert to any pattern that doesn't support our highest good or the highest good of those around us. Explore the ways you interact and react, behave and think. Do you always end up in arguments about the same issues with family? Do you have triggers that set you off, making you angry? Do you do certain things that end up hurting you, yet you do them anyway? Here are some common examples:

- "When I stay up late too many nights in a row I end up sick."
- "I have to get 8 hours of sleep, or else I'm useless."
- "If I wait too long to take my pain medication, I end up laid up on the couch for two days."
- "When I spend time with family, I always walk away feeling like I'm no good."

Does your thinking limit you? Do you think you're not smart enough or clever enough to land a good job? Do you think you can never amount to anything because of the neighborhood or the family you came from? We'll explore ways to expand your thinking in Chapter 10: *Know Your Power.*

Consciously go through your day, watching each interaction, reaction, behavior and thought. Look for the ones that feel familiar because they happen over and over. Look for the simple things you do, and the assumptions you make, like believing you have to go to bed at 10:00 each night, or coming home from work and sitting on the couch and watching TV, or the gossiping conversations you have at work. Do they best serve you and others?

If not, change them. Frank and I are consciously looking at patterns in our relationship that could use some changes. The first new behavior one of us chooses doesn't always work, so we try another one.

First observe, then experiment with changes and see what happens.

Take a look at the balance in your life. What proportion of attention do you give to your mind, your body and your spirit? You may like the current weight you give to each, but if you don't have true balance, you don't have true health and harmony. Assess your balance carefully, and don't get caught up in judging yourself by society's standards.

You Are Never Alone

When you do healing work for others (and for yourself), take comfort in knowing that you are not alone. As long as you ask for assistance, you will absolutely receive it. There are always Angels and spirit guides present, helping you to heal. As you become more accustomed to experiencing energy, you may feel them moving around you and even moving through your body. They want to assist you in any way that they can.

Andrea and I did Reiki together on our friend, Shonda, who had been diagnosed with cancer. Unbeknownst to Shonda and to me, Andrea had asked for our Angels to come and assist us. I had just started doing Reiki on others at that point, and it hadn't occurred to me to ask anyone to assist.

At the end, we shared our experiences with the session, and Shonda said, "At one point, you (Andrea) were at my feet and you (Wendy) were over here." She touched her left side. "But I felt another set of hands over here," and she indicated her right side. Andrea smiled and told us what she had done. Of course, from then on, I have always called upon the Angels, guides and Ascended Masters to help with my sessions. Since then, a number of people have reported the same phenomenon. Now I consistently feel presences with me. I'll often see colors and feel vibrations indicating that Jesus and Archangel Michael are present as I assist others.

More and more, I see Angel energies around my clients during my sessions with them. Any time I am fairly quiet and still and focused on someone for a few minutes, I begin to see who is with them.

I had an instance of rapid heartbeat where I started to say, "Jesus, please calm . . . " and before I could say, " . . . my heart," I felt an energy move down my face and into my chest and my heartbeat stabilized.

Always remember: Ask and you will receive.

The Importance of Human Form

Not only are you never alone when assisting someone with healing, but in fact, Spirit operates more effectively if it can work through someone in human form to heal another. This lesson had a big impact on me. It showed me how important we, in human form, are and that we need to stop thinking of ourselves as powerless.

Julie and I were told that we needed to go to the bedside of a hospitalized friend. There, Jesus appeared to both of us as we were putting our hands on our friend, to heal him. Jesus placed his hands on Julie's shoulders and energy began to flow from his hands down through her arms and hands and into the man on the bed. It was confusing. Why didn't Jesus just send the energy directly to our friend?

When Julie asked, Jesus explained that it is easier to manipulate matter when you are in the physical realm. For example, we can easily turn on a switch to turn on the lights. But just to flicker a light is a big deal for Spirit.

Shortly after, Jesus showed us how to consciously pass his high resonance spiritual energy through our own material bodies and direct it toward another. We now call this "The Jesus Energy," and it's available for anyone to use for the highest good. I believe this concept would work with any Avatar you would like to work with.

- First, imagine Jesus standing before you, just off to the side. You don't need to have a clear visual image; he'll be there by virtue of your intention.
- Imagine a beam of light emanating from his whole chest and flowing into yours.
- Feel it there. Give it a moment to gather.
- Direct that beam to the person you are working on and let the energy flow.
- Consciously cut the connection between you and the other person with your intention when you feel like it is enough— typically not more than a minute or so.

Be careful initially and don't overwhelm the person. Observe their reaction to the energy flow. I first used this technique with Shonda, my friend with cancer. She immediately flushed and said her heart was beating rapidly. I cut off the flow and she immediately felt much better.

When I asked Julie to ask Jesus for guidance about the incident with Shonda, Jesus told her that Shonda's body was, in a sense, broken and therefore not capable of holding the amount of energy that I sent. Jesus cautioned me to go more slowly until Shonda could hold more. I did this by imagining a smaller beam of light connecting my chest to Shonda's and cutting it off as needed.

When I tried The Jesus Energy on a few other people, it initially provoked symptoms in an area they were having difficulty with. Some felt short-lived sadness; others felt anxiety. When it was tried on me, I felt energy in my chest and a calmness.

You Can Help Others to Heal

Please know and believe that *you* (yes, *you*) have the ability to heal. You are a healer. You can heal yourself and you can heal others. When you believe this, you can heal with your hands, your presence and your thoughts. When you operate from love and exude love, just your vibration can help others to heal, if they are willing to receive that love. Whether or not you are attuned to Reiki—or another healing energy—you can heal with your hands.

Andrea and I were giving Reiki treatments and teaching Reiki classes together when Tracy and Paula came to us as clients. They listened to our personal stories, so they knew that people were capable of healing through their hands and of receiving information through hands-on contact. I believe that helped them in their own early experiences.

Even before she was Reiki attuned, Tracy felt heat in her hands and so did her brother-in-law. Then they found out that he had cancer. In the presence of his great need, she felt a profound desire to heal him, and it gave her faith in her ability to help him. She laid her hands on him, and they both felt energy pass through her palms. That's all it takes.

Paula, another friend, put her hands on her sick aunt before being attuned. She was flooded with information about her aunt's past that related to the cause of her present sickness. This was an early step in Paula's awakening, which inspired her to learn Reiki. Receiving information through hands-on contact is not necessarily a part of Reiki, but it does occur for some practitioners.

You can also heal through your aura. When my dad was in the hospital after having open-heart surgery, I am embarrassed to admit that I still felt uncomfortable about putting my hands on him. I was already a Reiki Master, but I hadn't shared many of my experiences with my parents. I was worried about how they might react. (I now know that I was wrong. They would have been fine with it because they would have wanted me to do anything I could to help him. They would have trusted me.)

What I did, instead, was to sit very close to him and pull energy through the top of my head, down into my heart and then I pushed it out into my aura toward him. I sat very close to the side of the bed, knowing that my aura was in contact with his and that I was pushing the energy into his aura and body. I imagined it totally enveloping and penetrating his body. You can also push energy through your heart chakra and guide it directly to their heart chakra.

Another way to heal is to just intend to visit the person in the nighttime, asking to heal them for their highest good and the highest good of all. My neighbor's kidneys were failing and the prognosis was that they would continue to fail. So I visited him regularly at night. His kidneys actually got slightly better and have not yet failed further, several years later. It could have been the nighttime visits. It might not have been. I love that because I can't take the credit for it. Ultimately, it wasn't me anyway; it was God working through me.

Remember, too, that prayer is energy, so you can help someone by praying for them. Science is beginning to validate the healing power of prayer.

We all have a variety of healing gifts. One of my gifts is the ability to take something from someone and run it through my body so that their problem is lessened. It seems to be heightened when my level of compassion is elevated. The first time it happened spontaneously, without conscious intention, when my compassion was intense. I was doing Reiki on my friend, who has a number of physical problems. She was helped, but the energy became stuck at my knees, and it hurt.

Here's the "recipe" for removing undesirable energy from others without holding onto it yourself. This was given to us by our guides:
- Fill your heart with love
- Feel confident that you will remove the problem
- Ask Spirit's assistance in taking it from the person
- Allow it to wash through you
- Wait to receive confirmation

Remember that you are only allowing the *thought form* to travel through you. If you do experience their pain, you are only experiencing the *thought form* of their pain, but you don't actually have their problem or disease. Having an indication of their pain or problem in your body will give you confirmation that their problem has actually passed from them, which does not always happen immediately. Stay out of the fear that you will get it.

I tend to ask for confirmations for everything, because the intellectual side of me wants to know, even though the spiritual side of me believes even without seeing. So I often receive some pretty crazy confirmations.

Tracy's dog, Bruno, was experiencing a succession of urinary tract infections. It was driving her nuts, because he would be up constantly in the night. She asked several of us to work on him long distance. I worked on Bruno and trusted that we had helped him, but wasn't aware of anything much happening in my session with him. Well, the next day as I was leaving my yoga class, the minute I hit the end of the yoga studio's long driveway, I was overwhelmed with the urge to urinate. I lived just five minutes away, but those were five of the longest minutes of my life.

I told Tracy that I was pretty sure we had healed Bruno's problem, because I had received confirmation! Sure enough, his problem proved to be gone.

Distant Healing

Energy practitioners learn to heal from a distance. You don't actually need to physically put your hands on someone. Everything is energy and energy is not bound by time and space. This is why prayer works. Your thoughts are energy that convey healing. Prayer brings additional energy from Spirit.

In distant healing, you are essentially working with an aspect of someone's energy, and giving it more energy, or clearing things from it. If someone is very sensitive to energy, they may feel sensations in the part of their body that you're working on.

There are several ways to do distant healing work. I do it by imagining an eight-inch version of the person standing in the palms of my hands. (I always think of the small, holographic image of Princess Leia from Star Wars.) I wait a moment and feel the energy as it arrives as heat and tingling in my hands. At that point, I begin sending healing energy. I typically move one hand around the person while keeping the other one underneath. Sometimes I'll use both hands. I feel for hot or electrical spots that indicate to me that energy is needed. If I know of a problem, I might focus energy on that specific spot, but generally I let the feel of the energy determine where I go. My hands will often feel pulled from one place to another. I send energy for as long as I feel is necessary, this is generally when the energy in that spot no longer feels different from the areas around it or when I can't feel flow through my hands anymore. Then I thank their energy for coming and send it back (See a specific technique for separating from someone else's energy in Chapter 12: *Clearing Energy*.)

I've had some amazing experiences giving energy in this way. One of the first was with Julie's daughter, Sami, who had a separated shoulder. As I allowed the energy to flow, I expected to be pulled to her shoulder. But I wasn't. I kept getting pulled to her feet. This confused me. I was in contact with Julie every day, so I knew there was no problem with her feet. The next day I checked in with Julie to see how Sami was doing. She gave me the update on her status, explaining how much pain she was in when they popped her shoulder back into place. I let her finish her story and there was no mention of feet.

Finally I said to her, "I just have to ask . . . is there anything going on with her feet?"

She said, "That's funny you should ask. She was in so much pain when they reset her shoulder that she clenched her toes so tightly that her feet ended up in tremendous pain!"

I don't doubt that her shoulder needed energy, too, but I believe that my guides used the situation to show me that I *am* able to accurately identify a problem. It also showed me that I don't always know what is highest and best for someone else. And I don't have to know. Because I can just trust my guidance.

I then quickly had three similar experiences. Tracy called me one night to ask me to send energy to a friend's father, who was being rushed to the hospital with a probable stroke. I requested that his energy come in between my palms in front of me and felt the familiar tingle and heat, but I could only feel it on his right side. In addition, I felt a pinprick of heat/pain hit my hand every time I passed my hand over the right side of his head. I interpreted this to mean that the stroke was in the right side of the brain and his left side was either weak or paralyzed. When we spoke a few days later, Tracy confirmed that this was true. I was beginning to get a little freaked and excited because I was generally not this accurate! My abilities were growing.

The next two experiences involved my friend Gary, who had been diagnosed with a recurrence of cancer and had begun chemotherapy. When I called in his energy, the field around his body felt much bigger than normal. My hands were pushed way out away from his body. I knew something was wrong. I sat with this a moment, energizing it and feeling the energy moving back into a normal size.

Then I realized that his entire body needed the energy because the chemo was coursing through his whole body, even though the cancer was confined to a specific spot. When I called his energy back a few days later, I expected to feel the same thing. Instead, my hand was pushed way up above his head. I energized this area and waited to be shown what was going on. I then remembered that this was the spot that relates to higher purpose. The cancer was likely there to help him figure out and hopefully step into his life purpose. Sending energy to that spot would help him to do so.

This is just the tip of the iceberg regarding my stories about distant energy work. Any intuitive energy practitioner who engages in distant work will have similar examples of having knowledge of a person's problems without having been told or without even having ever met the person. I like to work in the dark while doing distant energy work because I now see the energy coming from my hands. It appears in two different ways. It looks like sparks of light and mini lightning bolts. It's my own light show! I still marvel at it.

Keys for Healing

So keys for healing are:

- **Put the body in charge.** Say, "Body, take care of this."
- **Ask for help.** Ask God and the Angels and any other higher beings to assist you. Ask others to pray for you, or to help you in some way.
- **Learn the lesson.** Ask to know the reason for the problem. Say, "Show me the lesson." Look for what the issue can teach you. Make appropriate changes.
- **Relax and surrender.** Give yourself over to God for healing. Say, "Show me what this looks like. I surrender." Don't quit, don't give up, but do allow. Allow for the healings, allow for the blessings. Allow for the possibility of the problem to pass. Do not hold onto it. Disengage from the collective consciousness that says what happens in cases like this. Listen to medical diagnoses and predictions, but also allow that you could easily be an exception to the rule. You are not necessarily like everyone else who has had this problem, because you are dealing with it from a different perspective that can easily

lead to a different outcome. Eliminate stress from your body and mind, because stress will hold the problem in your body. We've all felt stress tighten our bodies and hold the tension in. You are holding energy in that tight place and that energy can stagnate there. It needs to flow. You will also receive clearer messages if you just allow, relax and become quiet.

- **Be patient.** Sometimes we simply need to show faith that the healing is taking place. Keep the quiet faith at the same time that you pursue every option.

- **Pursue every option for healing.** Pursue those options that feel right for *you*. You may choose doctors, healers, medications, herbs, exercise, etc. All can be used in the divine plan to help you heal. Thank well-meaning relatives and friends for their advice, but never allow them to make your choices for you.

- **Be grateful for the gift of this problem**. You must need this experience in order to heal something or learn something.

- **Break patterns.** Look for patterns of reacting, behaving, interacting and thinking that do not serve you. Make an effort and set the intention to change those patterns.

- **Strive to create balance between mind, body and spirit.** Carefully assess whether any aspect of you is being neglected, and realign as needed.

- **Seek.** Seek answers, seek lessons, seek solutions. Explore your thoughts and dreams.

- **Use hands-on healing.** There are some incredible hands-on healers. They are bright, gifted and intuitive. They are all over. Once you enter into this world and look for them, you will find them. They are just waiting to share their gifts with you, and most will teach you how to do it, too.

- **Use "The Jesus Energy."** Open your heart to receive and direct the energy from an Avatar's heart.

- **Laugh and stay positive.** You can feel the lightness and the difference in your vibration when you are positive and laughing. Depression is a very heavy feeling. Staying positive can be quite a challenge, but it's very important. I find it helpful to view any symptom as a release of negative energy.

When I feel a "twang" in my knees, I say, "Thank you for releasing that energy. I didn't realize it was stuck there."

- **Believe you have the power to heal.** *Know* that you have the power to heal yourself. You have much more power than you ever dreamed.
- **Visualize positive outcomes.**
- **Pray.** Pray in any way that feels comfortable. Remember that all thought is prayer, so **keep your thoughts positive.**
- **Let go when it is time.** This "problem" may be helping you to make your transition to the spirit world. Be grateful for the time it gives you and your loved ones to adjust to the transition.

See additional keys for healing at the end of the next chapter.

In the words of Archangel Michael, as we received them: "Be well."

Chapter 9
Be Well

Additional Healing Concepts

So much that was presented for us to learn and experience seemed to fit under the category of healing. Consider these additional concepts as you clear your channel.

Onions

The tricky thing about being human is that we have layer upon layer upon layer of things that need to be healed. It's like peeling an onion. As you peel off each layer, you find yet another layer underneath to be healed. In Integrated Energy Therapy, a hands-on energy practice, you can actually feel the issues in the aura as a drag on your hand that the practitioner then pulls out and releases. Kathryn Rose, my IET instructor, told me that anytime you pull something out of someone's aura it will go away, but that it's possible that the next time you do IET on them, you'll feel something in the same place. She said that's because the next layer is presenting itself for healing.

For instance, you may clear a fear of public speaking, just to reveal a fear of sharing too much about yourself one-on-one. You may clear that fear and realize there was an event in childhood, at school, where you were made to feel stupid for something you said the first time you raised your hand in your first grade classroom. Beneath that, you may realize that you developed an underlying core belief that speaking out is dangerous.

I definitely experienced healing as coming in layers. I never knew I had so much to heal! I regarded myself as someone who didn't carry a lot of baggage. Yes, things happened in my life, but I worked hard to move beyond them and not to let them impact my life. But there were many things that needed to be healed.

Some things that we regard as positive about ourselves actually need healing. One good example is workaholism. Most workaholics consider this a positive trait. The workaholism might, in reality, reflect a lack of balance, a hiding from something.

I worked hard throughout the years to heal, mentally and emotionally, from the car accident. I was no longer mad or sad about it and I could see many good things that came into my life because of the accident. But my friend Brenda, a gifted psychic, told me that I had more to heal related to the car accident. I was not consciously aware that there was anything else.

I was frustrated because I felt that I had left that car accident behind me twenty years ago. I sat with her statement for a while, asking to know what might be left to heal. Soon after, as I was driving home from work, I was talking to myself out loud:

"How is this possible?" I asked myself. "How am I not healed?"

I went through a list of all the things that were improved. The physical pain had lifted, so I checked off physical. On the emotional level, it no longer saddened me, and I wasn't angry anymore, so I checked that off.

Then I switched to the mental part. I heard myself say something I always used to say when I talked about the accident: "Well, the accident taught me that I'm a mortal being."

Bingo. Some part of me was still holding onto an old belief that I'm a mortal being. But I don't believe that any more. Now I believe that we are eternal beings who temporarily spend time in a physical body. But still, that old belief needed to be released. I needed to let go of that false belief, and I did it in that moment. Then I felt a calmness and a strong knowing that it was done.

When I went out to dinner with Brenda again, I said, "How's the car accident looking now?"

She said, "It's gone. You're healed."

It's like an onion peeling. There are layers that we have no idea about. It's not simply healing physical things—we need to heal thoughts, feelings, behaviors, and beliefs, too.

Let it ALL Go

Let go of anything that stops you from doing what you desire to do for your highest good and the highest good of all, anything that stops you from being free and from following your divine life purpose.

Another thing I thought I had let go of was related to the loss of two pets. Our dog was run over by a car and our cat drowned in the sump pump hole in the basement. I thought I was finished grieving, but Julie was scanning my body one day and when she came to the part of my body related to grief, she said, "Why do I see you crying?"

I said, "I have no idea." I searched and searched for something I was sad about, but I couldn't find anything.

When she got to another part of my body she said, "I'm getting the sense it's pets. It's animals." It brought me back to that memory. Then I knew I hadn't fully let it go. Instead, I think I buried a piece of it down deep, below the surface. I spent some time with the memories of those animals and the emotions surrounding their deaths. I simply sat with the sadness and allowed it to come until I felt like it was all out.

I still have a couple things that need healing. My next move is to put my life fully in God's hands. It's not enough to know all that I do at an intellectual level. There are still issues like control and planning for the future that are hard for me to let go of, despite the fact that I don't know where my future is headed and I do know that my higher self has a plan. I believe now that what God has in mind for me is much better than what I could ever imagine or create on my own. I need to let go and co-create with Spirit. When I do that, I believe the next level of healing will take place.

Healing "Past" Lives

I had a mild fear of attack that was with me my whole life. It began as a common childhood fear of something in the closet or under the bed and someone chasing me up the basement stairs. No big deal; many kids have those fears. When I became a teenager the fear persisted, but I attributed it to the fact that our home was broken into twice. It persisted as I got older, and I attributed it to my being female and therefore, feeling more vulnerable. After exploring that feeling with an attempt to clear it, I realized I could not adequately attribute it to events of this life. I also had a discomfort when I would go into a Catholic Church. It would literally feel like I had something on me that I needed to shake off.

In one of my early sessions with Will, I asked him about this fear of attack. He said that it was tied to lifetimes of being connected to Spirit and being persecuted for it. In one of those lifetimes, I was a nun and I feared the persecution of the church and of God. The instant I heard this, I knew in the core of my being that it was true. All the fears were lifted and I never had a problem walking into a Catholic Church again.

Will said that many healers and people who are awakening to their true spirituality are dealing with their fear of persecution, based on experiences from other lifetimes. He reassured me that this kind of persecution won't happen again. It can't. The energy of the world has evolved to a different level. Since then, I've met many, many healers and others connected to Spirit who have an underlying fear of persecution. This fear is stopping many of them from stepping fully into their life purpose. For some, this is an ancient fear that they've carried through many lifetimes.

Other things have come up for healing from other lives. Andrea had a past life as a schoolteacher. Her students were killed in a fire. This explained why she always had children hanging around her in spirit form. A number of people who could see or sense spirit told her this independently.

We call them past lives, but I believe a more accurate term is concurrent lives since time is not truly linear as we experience it. These concurrent lives are often the reason why people experience odd phobias, deja vus and a sense of remembering people or things from other times. I think of it as a bleeding through from other lives, just as ink can bleed through from one page to the next.

Leave it in the "Past"
To heal your "past" lives, look at fears, worries, prejudices, guilts, shames or anything else that doesn't fit your experiences in this lifetime. You have to look very closely. What behaviors do you have that don't match this life? Andrea had a need to put all the knives away at night before going to bed.

She never understood it until she learned about having been attacked in another lifetime. At that point, it instantly made sense to her.

We carry many of the same traits and interests through multiple lifetimes. They don't necessarily require healing, but it may help to understand their origins. Julie was interested in dancing as a child. She was told by Spirit that she was done with that. Dancing had actually come from another life and she didn't need to do it again in this life.

I also had some guilt and shame that needed to be healed. It wasn't about anything that I had done, but the feelings were tied to me in energetic form. They originated in a lifetime when I was declared a witch and burned at the stake. The guilt was not from having done anything wrong, per se. The reason for being deemed a witch was for my connection to intuition and to Spirit. The guilt and shame that I felt was for choosing to follow that path and therefore causing my family to suffer for my choices.

If you had told me what I just told you, several years ago, I would have said that you were crazy. So feel free! If I hadn't lived it, I wouldn't believe it. But I felt the emotions lift off of me after I re-examined and re-experienced those concurrent lifetimes. Later I helped others to re-experience their own concurrent lifetimes, and they had similar reactions. Beliefs, thoughts and feelings that didn't make sense before suddenly did make sense, just having the knowledge of the concurrent life experience.

I would encourage you to explore the beliefs and thoughts and emotions that have no basis in this life for you. You don't have to have someone confirm for you what the past life was. That would be ideal, but just recognizing that it doesn't fit is a good start. Then you can begin to release and heal.

I would wager that all of us have something from another life to let go of. The choice is yours. You don't need to heal the other lives. If you do choose to heal things from other lives, just ask to be shown what needs to be healed. Watch what you are shown and decide what you'd like to do about it. Although past life regressions are very interesting and can really help explain a lot, you don't necessarily have to use that tool. Everything is available here in this life.

Perfect at Birth
Spirit told Julie that we are all perfect when we are born. Our task is to go through life getting as little garbage stuck to us as possible. We commonly

call this garbage "baggage." Baggage can be useful. It can provide us with a "valid" reason for not moving forward with some aspect of our lives.

If you've been hurt in a previous relationship, no one can blame you if you're afraid to commit. Your baggage might even "entitle" you to certain behaviors. People can explain away their nastiness, for instance, because they've learned not to trust people, because of events in their past.

What's your baggage? Are you ready to get rid of it, or does it give you comfort and excuses? The choice is yours.

Julie was talking to her uncle one day when a guide stepped in and wanted her to explain to him that he was essentially perfect. He had been born into physical form in a perfect state. The things that were appearing now for healing were things that he had picked up over the course of his lifetime, including belief systems and attitudes that no longer served him. Many belief systems are imposed on us by others, and we never question them.

For Julie's uncle, this also included events that he held onto, that he hadn't allowed himself to simply "walk through." It included physical hurts that hadn't entirely healed, because unresolved emotions were still connected with them. For him, as for many of us, it also included lifestyle and food choices that didn't best serve his physical body and were now taking their toll.

The idea of being born perfectly confused me at first, because I knew we were also healing issues from past lives. If we were born perfectly, then how can I have something with me from the past? Then I remembered that time is not linear, as we experience it to be. Everything happens simultaneously. So how then are we born perfectly but still in need of healing from another life? Once again, it's the bleed-throughs. These are still aspects of you and sometimes you pick up issues from another you, and vice versa. Healing that part of you helps you to heal in the other dimensions as well, since energy is not bound by time and space.

How Fast Do You Want to Go?

I'm constantly asking to be shown the next thing that needs to be healed. I'm not sure I would recommend that approach to everyone because sometimes it hurts. There are physical pains that come up to the surface to be released from deep tissue. There is emotional pain that comes up for release. It's a positive process overall; you feel lighter ultimately and you become better able to be in clear contact with Spirit. Your vibration lightens so you feel Spirit more as you become less dense. But it can hurt. It hurts on different levels, and asking for one lesson or healing after another may keep the hurt going. Be aware of what you can handle.

I have made the decision to move as quickly as I can handle, and I requested Spirit's help in determining that pace. I reserved the right to change that decision at any time! I came here for a reason, and I want to move as far as I can on that path. I ask, though, that I remain balanced, and that I not focus too much on the spiritual and forgo the joy in the physical which is such an integral part of this life as a human.

When looking for what needs healing, look at the traits that appear positive and question whether they really are. You may want to consult with a trusted friend or mentor. You might say, "I have this thing that I really value about myself, but is it really a good thing?"

I don't know a workaholic who wants to give up working so much, but the people around him or her can see that it's too much. There's no balance and other things are missing. It's not healthy but it's hard to see from the inside. So you may want to enlist some outside help and, of course, ask for help from the Angels and from your own higher self.

Decisions and Exit Points

Apparently, we make decisions about whether to be sick and even whether to live or die. We all have exit points. Being in a physical body, as you know, can be very difficult at times. We are very light spiritual beings and the physical body feels very dense. So we are given exit points that we can use, to leave the physical world. You may be able to identify an exit point that you already had and didn't take.

My friend Maria was going through a health challenge, and she was in the hospital for some tests, but it was unclear whether there was anything seriously wrong. Julie told Andrea and me that we three went together one night, in spirit form, to talk to Maria and we convinced her not to be sick. But it was her choice; she chose not to take that exit. The next day, the doctors revised their tentative diagnosis, and she ended up having a minor surgery.

Tracy remembers an exit point well, because it was the most traumatic event of her life. During a camping trip, when she was just seven, she and her friends sat around the campfire chatting, and she remembers saying, "The one way I'd never want to die is by drowning."

The camp was at the edge of the lake, and the next day, while Tracy and her two friends were swimming into shore, a third friend was in a rubber raft. Tracy got caught under the raft, so she was pinned to the sandy bottom, unable to move or breathe. It took the girl in the raft a minute before she realized that she was on top of Tracy.

Tracy believes that, when she said she didn't want to die by drowning, she was rewriting the ending to the lake episode.

Astral Travel

I have had many experiences of astral travel. You probably have, too, but perhaps you didn't realize that's what was happening. Examine some of your "dreams" more carefully and you'll probably begin to see that some of them were actually astral travel. These experiences tend to feel very real, very vivid. The next morning you may remember having had a conversation with someone, but you don't always know what it was about. Astral travel is probably what has occurred when people say to you, "Hey, you were in my dream last night and it was so real."

Julie, Andrea and I had a couple of experiences where one of us visited another at night. It wasn't a conscious thing, but we would show up to talk or to heal. Then the three of us decided to make it more intentional. We would intend to travel at night to visit someone in particular, for the purpose of giving healing or comfort.

As I said earlier, if I hear of a need during the day, I immediately set my intention to visit that person at night, to lend assistance, if they want it. I say out loud, or to myself, "I intend to visit so-and-so tonight for the purpose of giving healing (or whatever I think they need) for their highest good and the highest good of all. They may accept or decline."

I then take it on faith that I will visit that person. I don't always ask for permission. Some energy practitioners are adamant that you need to ask permission to heal, or you are taking away that person's freedom of choice. Will told me that he has never had anyone's higher self decline assistance. I add the final statement, that they may accept or decline, just to make sure. It feels very right to me to attempt to assist.

Julie told me on one specific occasion that I had visited her and her daughter, Sami, to provide healing. I had set my intentions earlier because she was sick, but Julie didn't know, and I had forgotten. Julie experienced my visit that night, but I was not aware of it.

Just recently I received my own confirmation of nighttime healing visits. Andrea was complaining about having a knee pain for several days. I offered to visit her that night for healing, and I immediately set my intention to do so.

That night, I had an astral travel experience. I was working on Andrea's legs with my hands, and we were laughing and joking like we had been that day at lunch. In fact, it seemed as if we just continued where we had left off. It lasted only briefly, and I forgot about it until she called me the next day.

I said, "Hey, I visited you last night and I know it this time! I saw it!"

She congratulated and thanked me, and then paused and said, "Hey, my knee doesn't hurt anymore!"

We were both so excited!

Later, Tracy asked me where free will came in, if you were healing someone in the realm of dreams. I believe that Maria actively participated in her own healing, from a higher self perspective, because her waking self was scared that there was something seriously wrong with her. Regardless of the realm, if she didn't want the assistance, she wouldn't take it.

Transitional Opportunities

Illness can also be an opportunity to transition (to pass from physical form). It can give you and your loved ones the opportunity to adjust and say goodbye. When someone dies in a car accident, people will comment that it was so sudden, it came out of nowhere, and it was hard to adjust to their loved one's absence.

Obviously, it's difficult to watch someone die, but I think that if we have the outlook that it's a transition, this can make it easier. We're all going to transition at some point. Remember that the soul *is* eternal. But the body is not, and we can't take it with us. So we need a way to make the transition, and illness provides this for us.

Additional Keys for Healing

- **Look for additional layers for healing once one layer is released.**
- **Heal past lives.** Look for behaviors, thoughts, beliefs and emotions (especially fears) that don't seem to have a place in this lifetime. Once identified, release them.
- **Release your baggage.** Look for the justifications you have for dysfunctional behaviors, thoughts, beliefs and emotions. Seek to change them.
- **Enlist the help of others in identifying dysfunctional aspects of yourself.** But always seek your own guidance, and don't feel bad if you don't follow the advice of others. Don't give your power away.
- **Look for the positive shifts that illness may show you to take.** Make those shifts.
- **Use all realms, including dreams and astral travel, for healing.**
- **Take advantage of time provided for transition to say goodbye.**

Chapter 10

Know Your Power

You Are Powerful

The corollary to "Know your power" is "You have no idea how powerful you are." This is one of the lessons that humanity must learn in order to further progress in our spiritual evolution. We need to know our true power. We place such limits on ourselves and it's time we begin to recognize what we're doing and let go of our limitations.

Watch out for self-limiting thoughts like, "I don't have enough," "I'll never have that," "You can't beat that type of cancer," "I'm not good enough," "Hands-on-healing is ridiculous," "I'll have visible signs of aging as I get older," "I can't regenerate my body," and so many more.

There was a period of time when I kept receiving the thought to "Know my power, know my power, know my power," and to fully step into it. I really didn't understand what this meant. I was coming from the perspective of living in the concrete world, and my inner voice was encouraging me to step beyond my perceived limits.

Reiki had removed a significant limit for me. Before that, I would have said that it was not possible to heal with your hands. You cannot feel someone else's injury in your hands. But now I know that you can. It changed my life.

I began to explore this area of knowing your power. I created a list of all the things that made me think, "Wow, it would be so cool if we could do that." I also added some super powers to this list. My list included things like the ability to

- Talk to someone else's higher self
- Heal instantaneously
- Stop the body from aging
- Communicate via telepathy
- Manifest material things
- Eliminate physical pain
- Hear Angels
- Talk to Spirit without being in a state of meditation
- Know what other people are thinking or feeling
- Discern lies from truth
- Eliminate fear
- Create world peace

I began to disconnect from the mass consciousness that says that these things are not possible, and to adopt an attitude of, "If these things are real, show me." And incredible things started to happen.

We Are Powerful

We received five formal channels. We were reminded from the first channel that we—that is, all of humanity—were powerful. In the first channel, they told us, "You are all more than you know." In another, they said,

> Go forth into your next step with the confidence of who you are. Fear not the unknown, for it is you that is writing the results. Take care of your worries and put them in a place of small consequence. Do not choose them as your destiny. You hold the power and therefore you decide. Andrea, do not fear tragedy for there is no need to experience tragedy to grow. You do not need negative experience to grow. Look to the other side for guidance, but recognize that your power is here, within you and all that you do.

Andrea had a tendency to believe that we *needed* negative experiences for the soul to grow. I loved that this belief was not true. They also reminded us that we have all the answers. Spirit is there if we need help, but really, we have all the answers within us. How powerful we are!

Spirit called the second channel a "Rooftop Message." I think it was meant to be shouted to all people:

> *Today is an important day. More than ever your purpose has been realized and your gifts to the world are showing through you. We made it through a very special time and your message is to understand your power. Recognize the value in what you are doing. Go forth into your light and the knowledge that you hold great power in your hands. It is through all of you that you manifest your next step and the guidance we provide is only to further support your own plan. Realize your special truth and move toward the greatness that you deserve. It is through you that all are manifested and begin to grow. Hold on to your dreams, even those that no longer seem possible, for these hold the power of your next plan. Hope for the future and will the way of the truth to its new frontier as only you can do. It is with great love that we pass these words along to you. Recognize your power in all that you do. Hold not to the past, for even greater things are to come. Be well for now is the time.*

The channel was from Archangel Michael. The message here was that before we could do anything, we needed to change our mindset and understand what we were capable of. So that was what we began to do.

It was a reminder not to limit ourselves, because we do hold great power in our hands. It talked about manifesting and I have come to know that we do have great ability to manifest things in our lives. We can bring about things that we desire. If we put enough thought or fear into something that we *don't* want, we can create that as well. The conditions are right energetically for even quicker manifestation than has ever been possible.

Both of these messages tell us that our main power comes from within. Spirit is there in a supportive role and we can ask for help as needed. But our true strength lies within. I know some of you are saying "&%#!, then I'm really in trouble!"

For many, the statement that "our true strength lies within" is blasphemous. We're told God is outside of us, and without God we *are* nothing. Without God we are nothing, but God is *everywhere*, right? Isn't it blasphemous to think God is *not* within us? How is it God can be everywhere *except* within us? What makes you more (or less) special than the trees, the animals, the Earth or the Universe? Look within and find God.

The channel also tells us to hold onto dreams—do not give up on them—because you do have the power to make them happen. Do not worry about the past. What you have or have not accomplished does not have any bearing on what you are capable of accomplishing in the future.

I am reminded of the words of Jesus: "Truly, truly, I say to you, he who believes in me will also do the works that I do; and greater works than these will he do."[1] He taught us that we should not even be limited by *his* life, as great as it was.

Most Christians assume we cannot do the things he did. "Manifesting something from nothing? You're insane." If you believe in Jesus, then truly believe in his words. He said you can do what he did *and more*. Believe it.

Break from the Collective Consciousness

The big important first step is to break from collective or mass consciousness. Collective consciousness is our society's belief system. It was a turning point when I sat and created the list of abilities I wanted to have. It didn't mean that all those things happened instantly, or that I'm not still working to create many of them. But it did mean consciously breaking from the limitations that society has put on my life, and my behavior, and my expectations. It meant questioning everything I was thinking, saying and believing, and everything that others were saying.

Another important part of creating the outcome you desire is to notice when you're saying things that are limiting: "I can't do that because I'm not flexible enough," "I can't make enough money because I'm a speech pathologist and there's a limit to what a speech pathologist can make," "The doctor said I will probably get arthritis in my knees when I get older." The list goes on and on.

Watch your limiting thoughts. As an experiment, begin listening critically to everything others are saying, as an observer, and note when they are saying something that's part of the collective belief system. It happens constantly.

Manifesting What You Desire

Your thoughts and desires allow you to manifest things. Manifesting is bringing something toward you; creating something in the physical world through your conscious intent. You have the power to manifest what you desire. Place no limits on what you desire, because Spirit will often give you more than you would have requested. Your thinking should be "This or more; this or better."

Frank and I decided to move to a bigger house within our town, to take advantage of the excellent real estate market. We already lived in a wooded area and loved it. We knew we wanted to keep some of the rural feeling, which then ruled out a lot of the homes and neighborhoods in town.

A new house was being built on our road. We watched with great interest, and started walking through it as it neared completion. We struck up a deal with the builder, and had a handshake agreement to buy the house. Unbeknownst to the builder, however, his sister-in-law, who was the realtor, also had a potential buyer. Subsequently, our deal was pulled and I was absolutely devastated. I cried for two days (okay, maybe three!). I couldn't figure out why we lost the house.

We then shifted our attention from moving, and decided to do some work on our current home, with the thought of staying. A few months later we decided to look again. We found a beautiful house in an area that was wooded, so it provided the seclusion that we wanted, yet it was in a neighborhood, where the kids were closer to friends. In fact, Frank and I knew the parents of those kids, so we all had instant connections. This house had a pool, a hot tub and a deck that the other house lacked. It also had a sitting room off the master bedroom that I would use later, to write.

I already knew this neighborhood. About four years earlier, I dropped my son, Eric, at his friend's house which was across from what became our new house. As we pulled into their beautifully wooded driveway, I said to Frank, "You know what? I could live here. I love this neighborhood."

The house I previously thought I wanted was not good enough for Spirit. They knew there was a house that actually suited us better! But I needed to go through the disappointment of losing the first house. I didn't yet understand that there is always a reason for everything. So I took it very hard.

It ended up being one of a handful of pivotal experiences that showed me that everything is perfect. When it appears that I have not manifested what I was looking for, it's just a matter of waiting for things to align and not being too attached.

I then consciously tried to apply this lesson to each new situation. I renewed my commitment to surrendering to God's will. I would let God show me. But I still periodically became sad when things didn't go according to my little plan.

I've been in a period now where a few seemingly very "bad" things have happened, but I've been able to maintain my calm, without fear. Want to talk about power? That is real power: walking through the difficulty, while knowing that you are supported and everything is fine. There is no stress, no fear, no worry.

For example, in some of Frank's business dealings, he's been shown corruption in others. It resulted in unexpected financial losses, which produced great fear, anger and worry for Frank and others. Immediately and without conscious thought, I pulled back and did not get caught up in any emotion or judgment about the situation. It was so empowering. I was in the situation, but not of it, to paraphrase Jesus' words. I watched what was happening. But my experience was vastly different than it had been in the past. With time, I was able to see the beauty in bringing the corruption to the surface and removing it, instead of having it persist but remain hidden.

Back to Manifesting

Frank encouraged me to take a leave of absence from work, to be able to help out a number of family members who were having medical problems. I was concerned that we could not afford to have me out of work, since he had recently left his steady job to pursue his own business. He convinced me that we would be okay, because he still had his severance package and it was more important that I do the right thing by my family. Shortly after we made that decision "on faith," he remembered that he had received a bonus before he left work that was essentially equal to what I would have made during that time period. God provided what we needed before we even knew we needed it!

Spirit has been telling us repeatedly that we are all manifesting things very quickly now. So it is more important than ever to watch our thoughts.

If you are thinking negative thoughts, those things will come flying toward you. On the other hand, if you are thinking positive thoughts, those things will come to you very quickly as well. This speeding up in manifestation has taken place in our lifetime.

Julie was given the word "quicksilver," which is mercury. She was seeing the mercury falling by drops as if it was dripping down a tube and then being caught by a stream of air and shot off to the side. The message was that our thoughts are coming and then—boom—they are manifesting. It is so important to watch your every thought.

Be in control of your thoughts because you do have the power to "Ask and it is given." I said before that prayer does not just start at "Dear God" and end at "Amen." It is your *every* thought that He is listening to. So if you are thinking thoughts that say, "I am not good enough to get a job," you will not be good enough to get that job. Those thoughts must be changed.

Andrea and I were often reminded to change our thinking. Andrea was repeatedly given the message that "thoughts and words are powerful." For days, she could not get it out of her head: "thoughts and words are powerful." I was shown the number 51 repeatedly. The message of 51, according to Doreen Virtue's *Angel Numbers* is to think positive thoughts. It would typically come when I was thinking about a negative outcome. I was given this gentle reminder to change my thoughts.

Growing in Power

At one time, Andrea and I both had a ton of light bulbs burn out at home. I forget who mentioned it first and the other one said, "No kidding, mine are out, too!" We didn't think much of it. Of course, Frank the engineer said, "Well, most bulbs were put in at the same time, so it makes sense that they would burn out at the same time." Again, you can always look for the concrete explanation of things. But a short while after the first bulbs were replaced, I went through another cycle of bulbs. About this time, a pipe in Julie's basement burst and they had a lot of water damage. She was told, "As your power grows, things that are weak around you will break."

Another indication of our growing in power was that animals were being drawn to us, kind of like Dr. Doolittle. Squirrels and rabbits were getting so close that it felt like they were going to jump into our cars. I was minding my business outside one day when I was stung by a bee. I was so frustrated because I wasn't doing anything to upset the bee. I said, "Ok, if everything happens for a reason, why did that just happen?" I was told that the bee was attracted to my light and my energy. Since then, I've since been stung four more times under the same circumstances.

Frank and I were driving in the car. We weren't going very fast, and we had just turned a corner when a huge buck hit the front fender and rolled down the side of the car. It was the same kind of thing as with the bees. On another day four birds flew into my window! I had been sitting in that same office, at work, for years and nothing ever flew into my window. It was so bizarre because it was so out of the ordinary.

Warping Time

We have had experiences where it felt as if time slowed down or jumped ahead. I have woken up at one time in the night, and then woken up again at an *earlier* time. I would look at the clock saying, "I'm *so* sure it was later than this, the last time I woke up." You can't prove anything, because you've been sleeping and you may have just been groggy or dreaming. But I never had this experience before, back when I lived only in the concrete world.

On more than one occasion, I saw that I was going to be late for work. Oh well, I just resigned myself to being late—there was nothing else I could do (or so I thought!). Then I arrived on time. There was no way that could have happened. I took the same route to work for years. But it did. Others had similar experiences.

Time to Heal

It took nine months before the pain in my knee was fully gone. Torn menisuses are not supposed to heal. Conventional medical doctors say that they get worse until you have surgery. I had that experience with my right knee, from the previous accident, because I hadn't learned that we have the power to heal ourselves. Then, when I injured my left knee, I used Reiki and other forms of healing until the injury was gone. In fact, my left knee is totally healed now, while my right continues to give me a little trouble.

I think that first step of changing your thoughts and setting your intentions is so important. Watch thoughts that say things like, "Every fall and spring my allergies are terrible," or "My arthritis is worse in the winter." Remember: your subconscious is listening, and it hears your thoughts as if they were instructions. After living through major neck and back pain, year after year, I began to wonder what my life would be like at the age when *everyone* begins to experience aches and pains? Reiki changed my thinking about all that, and lo and behold, I rarely have pain anymore. When I do have aches or pains, I can make them go away through various methods. I have also stopped thinking that age has to bring aches and pains. It doesn't. See chapters 8 and 9 for much more on healing.

Miracles and Mother Earth

We are all capable of creating miracles. As our interest in helping others and our compassion increase, and our judgment of others decreases, our ability to create miracles is manifested in more tangible forms.

Julie was sitting in her backyard one day when she asked Spirit, "Okay, what can I do now that I have been flooded with this energy? Can I make the leaves fall from the trees?" A squirrel ran through the branches of the tree above her and sent a couple leaves and acorns falling to the ground.

She smiled and said, "Can I make that window open?" Her son Mitchell came to the window and opened it to ask her a question. She understood from that experience that she *could* cause things to happen, just by her thoughts. It was one more reminder not to set limits; we can do more than we think we can.

As you begin to recognize all the potential in using your own abilities to create positive change in yourself and others, consider creating change in nature as well. A friend of ours was staying at a beach house that Frank and I owned in North Carolina. I jokingly asked her to find a way to protect it from hurricanes, because she was there during hurricane season. The previous year's hurricane season had been bad, and we were living in the wake of Hurricane Katrina in New Orleans.

Once she was there, she received guidance that she could create a hurricane barrier by walking one-and-a-half miles in one direction from the house and coming back and then walking one-and-a-half miles in the other direction. This was actually six miles. She was told that she needed to do this for five days.

After the first day, they told her that she was doing it wrong. She was walking out the door and aiming at an angle down the beach. This would be natural. You typically would not head straight down to the water, and then turn left or right and walk along the beach; you would start walking at an angle in the desired direction. Then she would come back after three miles and take a break and head back up the beach later in the day, in the same manner. They told her that she was actually creating a funnel in front of the house! She had to go back out and aim straight down to the water before turning.

There was a hurricane reported while she was there, and she was going to have to evacuate early. On the final day, she did the whole cycle twice, which was twelve miles! It was such a wonderful, loving thing to do. Spirit told her that she would be able to see the barrier that she was creating if she looked behind her. She tried to see it during the first few days, but she couldn't, so they showed it in front of her. It was almost like train tracks that were intertwined, blocking the coastline. On the final day, she heard a voice she had never heard before. It was the voice of Mother Earth, thanking her for creating the barrier, because she didn't intend for the water and wind to destroy things. She said these were forces that even *she* couldn't control. What an amazing concept!

We had no hurricanes for the rest of the season. Coincidence? You are welcome to think so, but not me. The lack of hurricanes came on the heels of several years of bad storms.

Sharing Abilities across Lifetimes

I got the idea that if I am one entity, one spirit living in multiple bodies through multiple lifetimes, then I can tap into the knowledge that I had in all of those lifetimes. So I asked to know the healing abilities that I had during the time of Jesus, when my name was Rebekah. I asked for positive things that would aid me in my current journey.

Shortly thereafter, I went to visit my friend Karen who was in a bad state, emotionally and physically. I put my hands on her, and I had an incredible sense of compassion and empathy. We were kind of crying together, lamenting what was happening in her life.

Before that session, my knees had not been hurting. The moment I took my hands off of her and stood up, I had intense pain in my knees. I knew that I had taken something from her. I knew I had learned this from Rebekah. I was pulling it into my body, but it was getting stuck at my knees. It took four days to flush it through my body. I said repeatedly, "This is not mine and I do not accept it in my body. It must pass through."

Will confirmed that I was pulling aspects of Karen's problems through me, but I needed to allow them to pass. I needed to be very clear that they were not mine and that I was not willing to hold them in my body.

I had a similar experience after another Reiki session with Karen, but this time the pain only lasted for a day-and-a-half. I took an Epsom salt bath and the pain was relieved. I thought, "Okay, at least I'm getting better at this!"

I had been doing Reiki for other people in the interim, but it was only with Karen that I experienced pain. I don't know if it was the closeness of the relationship, or the intensity of her symptoms. I think it needed to occur, to show me what was happening and what I was capable of. We are all capable of amassing the tools from other lifetimes. There are no boundaries. Ask what the abilities are, and ask to be shown them.

Helping to Pass

I continued to ask to have access to abilities of other lifetimes. The following lesson came after several months of sensing that I knew how to help people transition from the physical world to the world of spirit. This thought became very persistent when I was asking to have Rebekah's abilities.

My grandmother was 98 and she was ready to go. She had an unshakable faith and was clear that she was going to heaven. She just didn't understand what was taking so long. When it was evident that she was dying, I made my plans to leave the next day, for Virginia, to be with her.

I sat in bed that night, wanting to help her to end her struggle. I said to her higher self, "Take from me what you need in order to help her to pass."

That night I had unbearable neck pain. This would happen to me from time to time; my neck would go slightly out of place, very high up. It seemed to come from sleeping awkwardly and stretching it out of place. But this night I had not even been to sleep. I couldn't put my head down because it hurt so much. I thought, "How will I ever drive five hours when I haven't slept, and I'm in so much pain?" But by the next day, the pain was largely gone and I had no problem staying awake and driving.

Over the next two days, I sat at my grandmother's bedside, talking to her out loud and in my head, telling her that it was okay to leave, that it was time and we were all with her. Yet she held on. There was nothing left of her. She hadn't eaten well for months and she hadn't had anything to eat or drink for the last two days. She was less than seventy pounds, and she looked like a breathing corpse.

I called Julie and she said, "Go to another realm and talk to her. She's afraid. Tell her that a part of you will go with her, and that you will meet her on the Other Side. Tell her you're already there waiting for her."

I spoke to Lindy and she said to put my hands on her "high fours" which are safety energy locks (in Jin Shin Jyutsu) at the base of the skull. She said that was where my grandmother needed to pull the energy from, to pass. So I put my hands under her neck and I went into my higher self and talked to her. Less than an hour later, she died. I felt like I gave her the extra boost she needed to finally let go and know that she was not alone.

On the way home, on my long drive, I called Lindy and told her that I hoped I helped my grandmother to pass, and I was sure my neck pain had something to do with it. She hesitated a second, and then said, "That was your high fours. Your grandmother was trying to pull the energy she needed from *your* high fours!"

I thought, "Oh, my God! I have to be so careful about what I allow to happen. She may pull *through* me, but she may not pull *from* me." It was another valuable lesson. I guess that the pain was worth having, in order to learn the tool. However, I once again respectfully requested that future lessons come without pain, but just as clearly!

Higher Self to Higher Self

Frank and I were involved in a lawsuit with a tenant who was refusing to pay rent. We were on the way to a deposition when I called Julie and said, "I just want her to do the right thing." She called me back a little later and said, "I just received the message that you should talk to her higher self and tell her to 'Know her heart.'"

I did as she suggested, and the woman didn't show up for the deposition, and subsequently didn't show up for any legal meetings. I felt there was a guilt factor related to her not showing up, so she was, indeed, in touch with her heart.

I went to see Wayne Dyer talk and he had Imaculee Ilibagiza as a special guest. She was a Rhawandan refugee who hid in a pastor's house as her tribe was being wiped out by a rival tribe. She wrote a book about her experience called, *Left to Tell: Discovering God amidst the Rwandan Holocaust*.[2]

On the stage that night, she told her amazing story of survival and faith. When she was finally able to leave that man's house, after an extended stay with little food and water, she encountered a soldier, who raised his weapon to her. She stopped and stared into his eyes while in her head she spoke to his higher self and told him, "You don't want to harm me; you are better than this." After a few moments, he put down his weapon and allowed her to pass. It was another confirmation that we do have this ability to talk to the higher self of another.

As Julie's abilities grew, there was no longer a line between the spirit world and the physical world. She was in constant conscious contact with Spirit and her guides, whether she wanted to be or not, because they'd continually butt in, even if not bidden. The worlds would bleed together, and she could not remember whether she had a conversation with me in this realm or another one. Now, she has become much better at keeping the two separate.

On numerous occasions, I talked to Julie and Andrea in my head and asked them to reach out to me because I needed them. Sure enough, one of them would call. On occasion, I'd have the thought to call one of them and she'd say, "I was hoping you'd call."

I'm sure you've had experiences where you randomly think of someone and, seemingly out of the blue, they call. This is because you have given them permission, through this other realm, to contact you. We all have access to this realm. Now you can expect it to happen with more regularity as you gain greater access to other realms.

Don't Give Your Power Away

Don't give your power away to anyone. You give your power away in a variety of ways. You give it away by not being true to who you are. You give it away when you don't trust your own guidance and rely too much on the guidance or opinions of others. Sharing too much of yourself with someone who does not respect the gift of who you are gives them power over you. Not recognizing your strength in a situation and acting from a lack of strength gives your power away. Doing or not doing something because of someone else's opinion gives power away. So does buying into the collective consciousness. My friends and I began to watch and remind each other when we were giving our power away, or not fully stepping into it.

Tracy used to routinely give her power away by undervaluing what she brought to situations and relationships. I frequently reminded her of all of her gifts and strengths. When behaviors were reframed in terms of giving away power, it became easier to identify and change them (for all of us).

Whenever I felt an Angelic presence, I immediately launched into my list of needs: "Help me with this pain." "Help me with this problem." Andrea admitted that she did the same thing. Then we received the message that we needed to ask, "How can *we* help?" We were giving our power away by assuming we had nothing to offer. By being here in the physical, we have the ability to influence people and situations through our presence, thoughts, words and actions. We need to believe this and act accordingly. I still don't hesitate to ask for assistance, but I also don't hesitate to offer mine.

I want to make one thing very clear about power. "Knowing your power" does not mean using your power against others. This is actually "force" as Hawkins describes it in *Power versus Force*.[3] Power, as I use the term, means being authentic and being who you truly are, at your core, and becoming who you are truly meant to be.

Most of us have to do some searching to discover who that is and, for many of us, it is revealed in small steps. Once one layer of thought, behavior or belief is released, another comes up for consideration. There is great strength and freedom in standing in your power, or your own true energy. Knowing your power also means discovering all your true abilities and using those abilities for the highest good. Recognize that your abilities evolve and change with time. Being open to your own change will facilitate your journey. Remember that you can call upon all the abilities that you have ever had in all your lifetimes.

Humility

I feel compelled to remind you that as you recognize your power and step into it, it's important to remember where that power comes from and remain humble. Our powers are gifts from God—the Divine. I believe that if you don't remain humble about them, they'll be gone. When you know someone else's thoughts or know what is wrong with someone, when you heal by putting your hands on someone, or when something shows up that you've been thinking about, it's easy to get caught up in your ego. You did it, but only because of the work you've done in clearing your channel, and surrendering to God, and allowing the Grace of God to come through you. Being a Clear Channel is essentially getting out of the way so God can work through you. It is putting your personal agenda aside, allowing the material world on Earth to be effected by the Spirit of God.

I always try to be mindful of the saying, "Pride cometh before the fall." I'm not willing to test that one. I love all of these new and exciting abilities and I'm grateful for them every day. I know they could be gone faster than they appeared if I don't appreciate them, remain humble and recognize their source. I know their presence in my life reflects a growing connection to God.

I've found myself close to tears on a number of occasions, after healing sessions where I was able to bring through some important information. I have literally sat there after my client has left, saying, "Thank you, thank you for using me in that way." I'm finding that as these abilities grow, so do my gratitude and humility. And as my gratitude and humility have grown, so have these abilities.

Multidimensional Beings

When you reincarnate, you are not simply dropping one body and picking up another body. Instead, you've expanded your immortal soul through many realms and dimensions. You are a being in many different "places" at the same time. You are powerful. Things are presented to you from another life because it *is you*. They are not being pulled forward from the past, but you might say they are being pulled sideways, since they exist simultaneously.

I've mentioned realms and dimensions, so what's the difference? I think of a *realm* as vertical and spirit-based and a *dimension* as horizontal and physical-based. My higher self is in another realm. I needed to project myself to that realm in order to communicate with my grandmother non-physically when she was dying. I think of this as going up. The Other Side is another realm, an alternate reality. Angels are in the Angelic realm.

For me, other dimensions are physical incarnations. I think of this as going horizontally *across time*. So . . . let's take this one step further . . . I know Jesus from another dimension—another physical lifetime where I am known as Rebekah. **And** I know him now as I connect with him in another realm for guidance, support and healing.

I recognize that this is likely a very simplistic way of conceptualizing realms and dimensions, but for now, it works for me.

This and More

The ideas and abilities described in this chapter are just the beginning. I know that with time there are things that you and I will do that I have not even thought of yet. So dream. Create your lists. Put no limits on yourself. Get rid of all limiting thoughts, because **you have no idea how powerful you are.** When you and I combine that power with gratitude and humility, then great and wonderful things will happen in the world. They are already happening.

Chapter 11

Divine Life Purpose

Live Your Joy

Human beings seem to be innately programmed to question their purpose in life, and to desire to leave their mark on the world—to make a difference. This is when we remember the Other Side of the veil where Spirit resides, where we know what our purpose is. But here on this side we tend to forget.

Instead of worrying about your purpose, I recommend that you focus on doing everything you can to become the clearest channel you can be. Work on healing your body, mind and spirit. Speak your truth, operate from love and know your power. Do these things and your divine life purpose will follow, because you will have laid the foundation upon which it can grow. Look back at the previous chapters and identify the work you need to do to.

You would probably like some things that you can be doing right now, to bring your purpose toward you, and not have to wait for all of this healing to happen, right? All right, I'll give you a few things to get started on. They are:

- Drop your ego
- Explore your gifts
- Live YOUR life.

Drop Your Ego

An important first step in finding your divine life purpose is to put your ego aside. Allow yourself to drop all judgments and expectations about what is good enough or not good enough to be a life purpose. Become open to being shown what you need to do, rather than pushing your ego to force it. Don't presume that you know what your purpose is. Don't expect to be able to begin your search and see your purpose right away. It might not be apparent yet. It may not be the time, because you have more clearing and preparation to do. Be patient and focus on healing. Don't let your ego force something into view that you're not prepared to handle.

Life purpose tends to come very subtly and quietly, as you begin to listen to your divine intuition and follow your abilities. Don't rush it. Just live your life and follow what brings you joy. It may be revealed that you are exactly on purpose and need to just continue doing what you are doing. Or you may be guided in another direction.

Sometimes you will be guided very abruptly, through an accident, or a trauma, or some change you didn't consciously choose. The change was chosen for you by your higher self because you weren't on the right path. So look very closely at any circumstances in your life that you would deem negative or unplanned. What can come out of those circumstances? What growth can occur? What activities will come from them? Where will you head because of this event? Begin looking at these events positively and drop the negative judgments that come from your ego.

Know that you are probably living on purpose already, or are at least on the right track. When I look back at the different circumstances in my life and the twists and the turns, they all led perfectly to where I am right now—to where I feel like I am absolutely on purpose. I don't know exactly where I'm headed. I know a few of the things that I need to do, and a couple of events that are probably coming, but I wouldn't presume to say that I can see my path clearly.

I do know that everything has been perfect—even the things that I hated. They were perfect to get me where I am now. When you can look at everything in the past and know that it was perfect, this can help you to look at the future, knowing the same thing. In fact, you can look at that "negative" circumstance in your life right now, knowing that there is something very important for you to learn. Perhaps there's an opportunity to learn that

- You are good enough
- You are lovable
- You are stronger than you thought
- You are worthy of love
- You are worthy of abundance
- You can find help and kindness in unexpected places.

Knowing that there is something beneficial for you in every situation that you encounter will help you to live more fully in the present, with no fear. Stop your ego from judging and know that all is well.

Explore Your Gifts

A key to finding your divine life purpose is to follow your abilities. What abilities were you given? They might appear simplistic to you:

- I'm a natural communicator
- I'm a good writer
- I'm a gifted gymnast
- People come to me with their problems
- Children feel very comfortable around me
- I'm cool in a crisis
- I'm compassionate when people are hurting
- I'm very flexible
- I'm good with money
- I'm at home in nature
- People look for me to lead and organize
- I see the beauty where other people don't

Look at all of them. They are not necessarily abilities that will produce a tangible product, but they might.

When my friend Karen was nearing the end of this life, she spent a lot of time wondering what her life purpose was. She had done very well for herself financially, but she felt like she hadn't accomplished anything meaningful. At one point, when I was deciding whether to leave my job and take time to write this book, she offered me financial support. She didn't understand the importance of that offer. If I am living on purpose, and if there is value in sharing this information, then her contribution would be huge—not just for me, but for the greater good.

But helping people financially was not something she valued because it came easily to her. She had the resources to say, "Go ahead and do what you need to do and I'll be here if you need me." She didn't think of that as anything special, but the offer was tremendous. It wasn't just the offer of money—it was her innate generosity—her willingness to use her wealth to support a worthy cause. Just her *offer* of support gave me a huge boost of energy and determination with which to continue. And that was a tremendous gift. Just because she didn't value her ability to contribute to people's lives financially didn't mean it's *wasn't* a gift!

That's what divine life purpose is all about. It doesn't have to be a big stretch. It doesn't have to be so out-of-the-ordinary for you. It's *exactly* who you are. That's the point. Why do you think you were given the skills and abilities and personality that you have? Because they are needed, meaningful and valuable.

Think about your abilities for a moment. Think about how you undervalue them because they're "no big deal" or you've always been able to do it. That's because God gave it to you and God expects you to use it joyfully! We think that our gift or purpose must be something that we have to work hard at, but it doesn't. **Doesn't it make sense that your purpose would align with your natural gifts?** (Imagine me shaking you by the shoulders while you read that last statement.)

Live YOUR Life

As you consider your own divine life purpose, I'd like to reinforce a point I made earlier. Please don't let society, family, friends, colleagues, acquaintances, strangers—ANYONE—stop you from pursuing your divine life purpose. It's not *their* life—it's *yours*. It's not *their* life purpose—it's *yours*. They're not receiving guidance about your life—you are. Therefore, they don't know what's best for you—you do.

Ask yourself if there is anything you're currently *not* doing because of what someone else would think. Are you not letting yourself date a certain person because of what your family might think? Are you not following your dream of a healing or arts job because it's not a "real" job? Are you not dancing freely at a party because someone might see you and think you look silly? The list goes on and on. Think about it.

Think about it very carefully and explore everything. You might want desperately to get up and sing karaoke at a nightclub, but you're too embarrassed to stand up and try. You can almost feel your body moving freely with the music as your eyes close and you feel the music coming out of you. But instead, you just sit there, because someone might laugh at you.

"So what? Big deal? What does karaoke have to do with my divine life purpose anyway?" you ask, mildly defensive. Well, maybe nothing. But unleashing your creativity, being comfortable with all aspects of yourself, expressing yourself freely in all forms and making the decision to live *your* life, free of the expectations of others, might have *everything* to do with your life purpose. Karaoke might be a venue that you're being shown, so you can take steps in that direction. Getting up on that stage may be the signal the Universe has been waiting for that says you are ready to face your fears and move into your divine life purpose. It may be the signal that allows the Universe to begin to open other doors for you.

That reframes karaoke a bit, doesn't it?

Consider and explore *everything*. See what holds you back and see where you're being led. Follow every feeling, every tug and nudge, and pursue your abilities.

When my grandmother passed at ninety-eight years old, she fought for a long time to hang on, even though she had been telling us for the past few years that she was ready to go to heaven. Her final three days were especially hard and you could see her determination to stay here with each labored breath. I couldn't understand why she was fighting so hard, when she knew where she was going and wanted to be there. Later, Will explained to me that she felt that she didn't accomplish everything she wanted to in this lifetime.

Don't let that happen to you. Gram was an incredibly active and independent woman, so I'm not sure what it was that she still wanted to do, and I cannot answer that for you, either. Only you know what you most desire to do. Go do it. Let the joy lead you, so that when you take your last breath, you will have no regrets.

The Flip Side

The flip side of "Live your life" is to "Let others live theirs." If you tend to be highly critical of yourself, you probably do the same to other people. Be careful not to impose your belief systems on others. Don't put restrictions on them and load them down with lots of shoulds and should nots. When people tell you what they're thinking of doing, try to listen from a position of non-judgment and openness. Be curious and creative. Help them to explore their ideas. This is *their* journey.

A good friend recently confided in me about a plan that could possibly cause him and his family some pain, because it involved revealing some things in his industry that certain powerful people wouldn't want known. I helped him to explore the situation from all angles, but refrained from giving my opinion about what he should do. It just might be that revealing inadequacies in the system and being a whistle-blower is something that he is here to do. I wouldn't want to interfere with that, despite the potential for pain. The soul wants to do what it wants to do, whether the physical self is comfortable with it or not. It was his decision to make, not mine.

Catch the Ball

Lindy went to a Reiki share (where Reiki practitioners get together to practice and give each other treatments). The person working on her told her she felt a ball of energy over her head, but she didn't know what it was. Soon after, Julie was told that she also had a ball of energy over her head. I was taught later in Integrated Energy Therapy training, that when you are becoming ready to accept your divine life purpose, it appears at your eighth chakra as a ball of energy. The eighth chakra is about three feet above the crown chakra (the top of your head). (See Chapter 1: *Energy* for an overview of the chakras). I was very disappointed that I didn't have one. We didn't even know what they were, but I wanted one because they had them!

Shortly after, Julie was told by Spirit that these balls were outside their bodies because they had not yet decided to accept their divine life purposes. Now I *really* wanted one! I was whining to Julie one day about not having one when she paused, looking at me quizzically, and said, "You took yours in a long time ago. As soon as it presented, you took it!" My ball was this book.

Lindy's purpose was to open a healing practice and step more fully into hands-on healing while continuing to teach yoga. She is now doing that, after clearing some initial fears. Julie thinks she knows what her ball is about, but she's waiting for the specifics to present.

Simple Plans

We tend to develop judgments about the worthiness and value of roles in our society. We tend to have expectations of what our life should look like, in order to be deemed worthy. At the spiritual level, a divine life purpose could appear very simplistic. It could just be to hold the vibration of love here on Earth. You may know several people who have an admirable ability to show unconditional love under any circumstances. Frank's Aunt Dorothy is an example of unconditional love in our lives. She is always there to do whatever anyone needs, with love and without judgment. She leads a wonderful, very blessed life. I believe that is at least one of her purposes—to hold the vibration of love and to be a model of unconditional love.

When Aunt Dorothy retired, she decided to volunteer at a home for unwed mothers. I was scrambling at that point in my life. I worked full-time, had two young kids, and Frank was on the road, out of state, most of the time. I struggled to get the kids home and fed, the kitchen cleaned, the dogs walked, etc., especially on Tuesdays, my late night. Aunt Dorothy offered to pick the kids up from daycare early and feed them. I eagerly accepted!

After a week or two, I realized that Tuesday was the day she volunteered at the home. I said, "Wait, it's Tuesday!" What are you doing here?" She humbly looked down and said, "My family needed me."

No fanfare—nothing! She saw an opportunity to help and she jumped in. I am very grateful. More importantly, my kids have commented on her example.

Another purpose is simply to hold energy. At the time of Jesus, many people around him held an energy vibration that enabled him to do his work. I imagine this occurred around all the great Avatars. Certain people maintained a vibrational level within themselves that allowed the Avatars to be effective. These people probably had no idea of the important roles they played. But that didn't make it any less important. The Avatars didn't do it alone. Even now, people are creating patterns of vibrations that can promote world peace, healings and compassion.

Another purpose may be to heal. Many people with serious health issues get caught up in thinking, "This is no life. I can't do anything meaningful because I'm so sick." They don't realize that learning how to get healthy, or how to cope with their illness, may be what their soul is here to do. It could also be that once you're able to do this level of self-healing, then your divine life purpose will unfold.

A dear friend of mine knows that her purpose in this lifetime is to heal her body. She has led multiple lives where she has had serious afflictions and has ultimately committed suicide in each one. She knows that in this lifetime, her purpose is simply to heal her body, so she has committed her life to this goal. In order to survive financially, she also dedicates herself to helping others heal. Most people would just recognize the latter (healing others) as important and would look at the former (healing self) as something that gets in the way of a more "legitimate" purpose of healing others. My friend has been able to realize that her soul actually wants to learn first how to heal itself.

So being sick and healing that sickness can be very meaningful. Our higher selves have very different ideas of what's important than we do!

It is my personal belief that our highest purpose is our own spiritual evolution; holding the highest vibration we can and heading toward enlightenment.

Show Me

For some people, the above purposes wouldn't be good enough. They want to feel like they're contributing in a very tangible, observable way. But these other *intangible* purposes are often more important than the things we can see. The desire to see the purpose stems from the ego.

You may know and even envy people who are living very much on purpose. They may be keenly in touch with their guidance. They may be artists, or nurturing mothers, or great CEOs.

Whatever your purpose is—grand or simple—you chose it before you incarnated, so it is meaningful. Don't judge it, because you can't see the whole picture; you can't see what's coming and you can't see where it's leading you. When I was injured and in pain for three years, directly following my car accident, I would look at my situation and say, "What's the point; what's the purpose?" I couldn't see the purpose. I needed to give it time to unfold. Allow it and don't force it, trying to make it look a certain way.

It could be that you're here to awaken people through your words or actions. You might not even know that it's occurring, but you may be giving others a tremendous gift. You may not be getting day-to-day acknowledgment of what you're doing, especially if it happened without you consciously *trying* to awaken people. You might hear someone occasionally acknowledge something in your behavior, like "It was really amazing how you didn't get frustrated in that situation," or "How great that you weren't provoked to anger by him," or "You always selflessly put your own needs aside to help others."

We frequently hear stories about a successful CEO or an inner-city kid who makes it big. Then thirty or forty years later, this person acknowledges his first grade teacher for believing in him, or his next door neighbor for making him believe he was worth something. Most likely, the teacher and the neighbor had no idea they were having such a strong impact on that child. They were just living their lives and doing their thing. I don't believe we know a fraction of the good we do on a day-to-day basis. You may have had someone come up to you and remind you about something you once said that had a huge impact on him or her, but you can barely remember having said it.

Follow Your Purpose

Be aware that your purpose may not remain the same forever. People often get caught up in doing something because it was right at one time. I have no doubt that I was supposed to work as a Speech Language Pathologist in a brain trauma facility.

But then the shift began. As I explored that shift, it became easier for me to let go of a job that once gave me such pleasure. When I left, I gave everyone a T-shirt that read, "Live Your Joy," in an effort to help them understand why I needed to go. I still loved them, and the clients, and valued what they did beyond measure, but the joy had moved, and I needed to go where it was leading.

That job led me to develop compassion, to understand trauma, and to learn how to talk to people. It led me to people and experiences that helped me in the next part of my journey. But I needed to leave. My spiritual contract had changed. If we follow our own guidance and intuition and Spirit's guidance, the change will be for the highest good.

Always stay in touch with the feelings, the nudges, the tugs and follow where they lead. Be true to them, no matter what. It doesn't matter if you walk away from a relationship or a high-paying job or something that looks very altruistic—if you're living on purpose.

Now, I wouldn't make those decisions quickly or take them lightly. You could just be getting the guidance that the relationship or job needs to shift in some way. You need to be sure that you're not just walking away because of some difficulty that needs to be confronted. Life will not always be easy. But what other people think of your decision should not matter, as long as you're living on purpose. You need to follow where it takes you.

I have a friend who left everything and went to write in Russia. Everyone thought she was crazy. But she knew that was exactly what she needed to do. It doesn't matter what other people think, because they're not receiving guidance regarding *your* life. Remember to respect other people's choices as well, because you're not receiving guidance about their life.

Pre-incarnation Checklist

To reiterate: before incarnating, we chose these lives. We chose very specific lessons to learn and outlined some events to help us learn those lessons. The events that happen in our lives, no matter what they are, are important. The more things that we experience from our Pre-incarnation Checklist, the more pleased we'll be with ourselves when we pass over from this lifetime. We'll say, "I did it and look at the outcome! It wasn't easy, but I did it." Or "They said I should have gone for the money, but look what I did instead." Or "I went for the money but I also acted with integrity." Always strive to be the best you that you can be. Remember to be quiet so you can hear Spirit, listen to Spirit, follow Spirit. Listen to your nudges, follow your abilities and you will be on purpose.

Purpose Plus Joy Equals Success

I've mentioned the importance of joy several times, with respect to life purpose. But joy alone is not enough for you to judge your life as successful, after you transition to the Other Side. You need to find your purpose as well. My guides made this abundantly clear when Karen, one of my dearest friends, passed.

Karen was very sick and very young when she died. I was feeling very sad and missing her so much, and I felt really confused and more angry than I'd care to admit. That was when Spirit pushed me to consider whether Karen had had a successful life or not. As far as I was concerned, their timing for this conversation, really stunk!

Honestly, I didn't know whether she had a successful life. She often seemed joyful; she could become so excited about the littlest things. So she had many happy times in her life. But she also experienced extreme sadness with great regularity, and she was in so much physical and emotional pain. So I didn't know. They kept repeating that there can be "joy in the pain, joy in the pain."

When it came to purpose, I was still confused. I saw tremendous purpose in her life *and* in her death, but she never did. As she neared the end, she'd ask me repeatedly "What's the point of my life?"

I readily listed all of the beautiful purposes that I saw, but she didn't believe me, because they didn't feel purposeful to her. I didn't think she needed to know the purpose while she was here, in order for her to judge her life as successful when she passed.

The discussion regarding a purposeful life and choosing to be sad led to this channel:

> Purpose plus joy equals increased vibration, because if you do your purpose without joy, there is little increase. If you are happy without purpose you are ultimately unhappy. If you have purpose without joy, you lose ground with repeated joyless lives despite purpose.

By losing ground, they meant that your vibration was decreasing.

So both joy and purpose are important, because having both will increase our vibratory level, which will allow us to hold more light and love.

That which you are supposed to do (your purpose) and that which you most deeply desire to do are one and the same, because you came here to do that work. That's why you feel the most deeply fulfilled when you are doing it.

If you keep doing something solely because it makes you happy, Spirit was telling us you ultimately will end up unhappy, unless it also brings with it a sense of purpose.

So to help you find your purpose, start by finding what makes you the most deeply happy, and then do it. If it begins to shift and you feel less joyful, then find the joy again and live in the midst of it. If you aren't sure what your joy is, then try out lots of possibilities. Don't judge them. It doesn't have to make money. It may turn out to be a hobby that brings you a deep sense of satisfaction. It might be something you volunteer at.

After thinking about all of this, I decided that Karen, on the Other Side, probably concluded that she had lived a successful life. She served others, was a loyal friend to many, and modeled how to love despite rejection. She had such joy in the little moments and there was much purpose in her life even though she never saw it herself. She had both of the necessary components. Allow yourself to feel the joy in what you are doing *in every moment*. If you're one of the lucky ones who have found your purpose, remember you're only half-way there. Choose to feel the joy, too. Don't hold back. Remember that you will judge this life as less than successful if you cannot feel the joy.

Chapter 12

Clearing Energy

Get Unstuck!

At the time of my father's open-heart surgery, I was given guidance that he was going to be absolutely fine. I knew this was true, yet I was sad that he would have to go through the severe physical and emotional trauma of having major surgery.

As they were wheeling him past us just before surgery, I felt calm as I leaned over and kissed his cheek, but when I put my hand on his shoulder, I was immediately flooded with emotion. I felt very scared and wanted to cry. I was taken by surprise. Why was I feeling so badly when I knew that he would be fine? As soon as I walked away, I could feel that it was not *my* emotion; it was my father's. I had taken on his energy. We take on energy through the emotions and physical pain of others.

Knowing how to clear energy from your body is important for maintaining a healthy body, mind and spirit. We are always taking in energy from other people and from our environment and, ideally, we are using what we need and allowing the rest to flow unimpeded through our bodies. The natural flow of energy into and out of the body is a good sign of health. As the planetary energy continues to change—through increased sunspots, changes in the electro-magnetic field and other ways—there will be an increased demand on your body to take in, assimilate and release these energies.

Occasionally, out of the blue, I'd have a very sad day. I'd find myself overwhelmed with sadness. These days were different from days when I was sad about something in particular. They were also different from the times I was in denial about a sadness I was feeling. These were times when I knew that I had nothing to be sad about. My family would notice my sadness, and ask, "Have I done anything to make you feel mad or sad?" They looked for some cause, as did I, but there was none. I could not attach it to anyone or anything.

Then I was given guidance that I was actually running things through me.

Symptoms

If you're taking on energy from other people or the environment, you might have an uneasy feeling. You might not be able to relax because there's too much energy in your body. You might have an increased vibration in your body that can feel unpleasant, distracting or overwhelming.

Sometimes when I have too much energy I feel giddy, and other times I feel disconnected from my body and make a lot of silly mistakes. Tracy feels too much energy as anxiety. Now that she can identify the anxiety, she can pursue ways of releasing the energy, rather than looking for possible reasons to explain the anxiety.

Most everyone has a weak spot where energy tends to get stuck. As I've mentioned, mine was my knees. I realized that there was a grounding or a clearing of energy that needed to happen. I began having incredible pains that felt like energy was stuck in my calves.

Another signal that there is excess energy is the feeling of restlessness in the arms and/or legs. The feeling tends to predominate in the legs. It fits the classic definition of Restless Leg Syndrome (RLS). It happens more at night, and if you get up and walk around, the discomfort will ease. But it may start up again as soon as you lie back down.

You might also have your own emotional energy stuck inside you. You may not have fully experienced and released an emotion. In that case, a good cry, or a few punches at a punching bag or pillow might help.

Techniques for Clearing

Here are some useful clearing techniques:

- **Feeling Emotion.** Simply feeling your emotion will help to clear the energy. Feel it fully and then let it go. We have all, at one time or another, tried not to cry. We hold it in. Feel your body when you do this. Feel the tightness and pressure. Sometimes it physically hurts your chest, arms or abdomen. Let the emotion flow instead. There's nothing wrong with feeling emotion. Emotion is natural in this human experience. Go ahead and feel it fully and then let it go.

- **Relaxation.** Relaxation helps open all the joints and muscles, to let the block break up and exit the body. Many of the techniques in this list can help you relax. Meditation, stretching and walking in nature can also help.

- **Directed Breathing.** Try breathing through a block in the energy. Inhale deeply and then direct the exhalation, with your intention, to the place that hurts or is uncomfortable. Blow the exhalation through that spot as if to push it or dissipate it. You can blow it out through the bottoms of your feet, your palms, or your crown chakra, depending on where the block is. The exit point closest to the pain seems to work the best.

- **Visualization.** Visualization is great for moving energy and relieving blocks. Visualize the area with the pain or discomfort opening up as the block moves through the body. You can couple this technique with relaxation and directed breathing.

- **Yoga**. Yoga optimizes the energy flow in the body by opening the chakras and meridians throughout the body. Yoga utilizes movement, postures and breathwork to produce a relaxed body and mind and a spiritual focus.

- **Acupuncture**. Acupuncture is a specialized technique which uses needles to open the meridians.

- **Epsom Salt Baths.** My favorite technique is to take an Epsom salt bath. The warmth is so comforting and relaxing! The water alone helps to equalize the energy, and the salt is energetically cleansing. Salt is used in many cultures for clearing negative energy. It helps to calm the vibration, pain or jitteriness. Sometimes I'll use it at night; it helps me to relax and go to sleep. **Read the packaging for restrictions before using Epsom salts.**

- **Reiki.** All energy practices help to clear energy from the body and the energy field. Reiki is very beneficial for calming the body and enhancing energy flow.

- **Jin Shin Jyutsu.** Jin Shin Jyutsu is another beneficial practice that focuses on placing pressure on key points to break up blocks and encourage flow.

- **Integrated Energy Therapy (IET).** Integrated Energy Therapy uses a different energy vibration than Reiki. One of its main techniques focuses on pulling negative energy out of the aura.

- **Meridian Clearing.** Clearing your meridians allows the energy to flow better. There are twelve meridians that run through your body, supplying energy to your organ systems and other parts of your body. Simply trace the line of the effected meridian a few times with your finger or crystal.

- **Crystals.** Crystals are a very old and effective way to open blocks. Obsidian is particularly useful for grounding and smoky quartz is useful for pulling negative energy out of the body.

- **Grounding.** Put your feet on the ground (preferably outdoors, but not necessarily) and let the energy flow into the ground. Bare feet on natural earth work best.

- **Burning Herbs**. The burning of sage, cedar and/or sweetgrass is a tradition used in many cultures for clearing energy. Wafting the smoke in the four corners of a room can be helpful.

- **Essential Oils**. Diffusing the oils of frankincense, sage, pine, lemon and/or angelica can be effective for clearing energy. One simple method is to put water in a spray bottle, then add a few drops of oil. Shake vigorously for a minute, then spray in the four corners of the room. You can also spray a foot or two over the heads of people. Spray over crystals or other objects that you want to clear, including beds and massage tables.

Clearing Another Person's Energy from Your Own

As a clairsentient, it's common for me to feel things during healing sessions. I'll say, "You're holding your anxiety in your abdomen—let's get it out of there." Or "Why am I feeling so sad? What's upsetting you?" Often I'm feeling the underlying reason for what's ailing them and it allows me to target it more directly. It helps me to know where to place my hands or what technique to use.

It's becoming more common for people to feel another person's energy. They may feel the energy in the form of the other person's emotion or pain. Empaths are people who can feel other people's energy. Many are challenged by being in crowds or even small groups of people. As more people are becoming empathic, I hear more complaints about people having trouble around others. They might experience more difficulty in places where emotions run high, like hospitals, funerals and courtrooms.

Feeling someone else's energy is not a bad thing, in fact, I personally consider it a blessing because it makes me better at what I do. However, it becomes a bad thing when you hold onto it and it impacts your body and/or emotions. Many psyhics have difficulty working for very long and some even become sick, because they have to "get inside" the other person's energy to be able to do their work. They don't even have to be in the same room or the same state as the person they are reading.

I just assume now that I have some residual energy on me following any healing session, so it's part of my routine to clear my energy when I'm done. I also clear my energy when I've been around someone who is particularly emotional.

Here are two techniques for clearing the energy:

Joy just holds her hands and wrists under cold running water for a minute or two. She says that energy follows water, and we are mostly water, which explains why we absorb other people's energies. But doing this will send the energy down the drain.

Will's technique encourages me to get back in touch with my own body, grounds me and connects me with my higher self. This procedure will work for any type of interaction with people and is especially recommended following a healing session.

- Center your consciousness at your heart and hold it at the center of your chest for a moment.

- Then move your consciousness up through your throat, then your third eye (between your eyes) and out the top of your head.
- Now take it all the way to the sun (imagine it leaving the top of your head and heading to the sun for cleansing). Hold it there for a few moments.
- Bring it back down through the top of your head, third eye, throat and back into your heart and hold it for a moment.
- Now send it out through your hands, feet and root chakra into the earth. (You have just cleared any energy that is not beneficial for you.)
- Now bring your consciousness back up into the center of your chest.
- (Next, it's important to completely separate energetically from the other person's energy.) Swipe your hands across each other, as if you are brushing dirt from your palms. Take your right hand and push it away from you, as if you were motioning to someone to stop. (This creates the intention of pushing their energy back to them.)
- Take your left hand and put it on your chest. (This brings your energy back to you, creating a separation between you and them.) Hold this for a moment. Feel your energy at your chest.
- (To close yourself up so you will not take on new energies again:) Start with your dominant hand in front of your groin, with your palm toward your body. Imagine closing a zipper as you move your hand up the center of your body, to the top of your head.

Finally, you can seal yourself off from someone specific with the following technique:

- Draw a figure eight in your head. Place yourself in one hole and the other person in the other hole.

Sounds crazy, doesn't it? But it works. It helps the *most before* you engage with someone. Once you're in the middle of an argument it feels too late to use the figure eight alone because your energies are already connected. You would have to do the clearing technique first.

Breaking Energetic Ties ("Cords")

A more significant connection to someone else's energy is called a "cord." People who can see energy literally see bands of energy that are like umbilical cords, going from one person to another. These cords are created through extreme neediness or maliciousness. They are used by one person to suck energy from another. Umbilical cords are appropriate when an embryo is helpless, but it needs to be cut when a baby can breathe. When a needy relationship ends, the person who was being corded feels like he or she cannot stop thinking about their former mate. It feels like a monkey on their back (or in some specific part of their anatomy). Once the cord is cut, there is an amazing sense of relief.

We need to be on the alert for negative energy ties that have the potential to be damaging and draining. One way to clear these cords for yourself is to use your hand in a swiping motion, like a windshield wiper, along the front of your body, in front of each chakra, to cut inappropriate energetic ties. You can also swipe across the top of your head and even down your back. You can also use crystals. Some healers use ornate, ceremonial knives to cut cords. You can also imagine a sword of White Light.

Learn how energy feels when it's stuck in your body and experiment with these techniques to find the ones that work best for you. Be alert to protecting yourself from other people's energies, especially before entering into a potentially argumentative or challenging encounter. Always protect yourself before and after a healing session.

Chapter 13

Support from Others

Don't Go It Alone

Sharing with others makes the good times better and the hard times easier. Reach out to others and help them along, and ask them for help when you need it. You might be able to enter into *Homo spiritus*, our next step to spiritual man, alone, but why would you want to? It helps to share your insights and experiences with at least one other person. But I'd find more if I could. Remember, we're all in this together.

Spiritual Family
From the beginning, Andrea, Julie and I had a feeling that we were supposed to be working together spiritually, and that we were some kind of team. Spirit always spoke of the three of us as a unit, and sometimes called us a "trinity." Will said he preferred the word "prism," because we were here to amplify each other and to amplify the energy of those around us.

Before Julie developed a clear, ongoing dialogue with her guides, she would occasionally receive a block of information through "automatic writing." She would feel guided to start writing, and the words would just flow out onto the paper, without any effort or thought on her part. These were very exciting times because, although the writings often seemed vague and obtuse, we knew Spirit was talking directly to us and that was an amazing feeling.

Each morning, on our way to work, Andrea and I waited eagerly, hoping she would call to tell us she had received another message. But it only happened five times. The writings stopped at the point that Julie was able to have an ongoing conversation with Spirit. Even though the dialogue was more effective, we missed the writings. The messages that Julie received were always for "the trinity." The guides reminded us from the beginning to reach out to each other. In the first writing, they said:

> "Recognize that the three of you have been doing more than was originally intended and that you have all been working very hard and we are grateful for your efforts. We have great love for all of you and it is through you that our work will also grow. There have been extreme changes. Recognize them and learn from them. All have had a great purpose, more than you can realize at this time. You are all family and it is by design that you have come together. Know that you are all loved and it brings us great joy to see you together."

So we knew that we were supposed to be working together and that whatever our purpose was, it was also important to Spirit.

In another message, we were told:

> "Now is the time for all of you to begin reaching out to your spiritual family daily over your normal routine. You must continue to develop your circle and recognize the Angels that are sent your way—there are many.

We began to recognize that all the people in our lives were Angels of sorts, placed there for us, as we were placed there for them. They were important, whether we liked their roles in our lives or not. We began to shift our views of people, especially the "problematic" ones, and we began to have fun looking for the gifts they were there to give us.

The writings also told us to enlarge our circle. Since we enjoyed each other's company so much, it would have been easy not to reach out further. But as we reached out, others reached back, and that enhanced our ability to interact and grow with others, and to touch one another's lives.

The message continued:

> "Do not forget to enjoy each day/your togetherness on earth. These were choices that were fulfilled. Connect with one another

frequently and receive and give strength. You are all Angels to
each other.

I needed that reminder to "enjoy each day," because I often got so caught up in learning that it would become like a second job. The idea that we chose to be together before incarnating was staggering.

Julie said, "What are the odds of all three of us choosing this plan before incarnating, and then actually making it here together, with all of the choices we've had in our lives? Think about it."

Spirit added:

"Squash fears and doubts. There is no time or need for this, for
you are manifesting even when you feel stagnant.

Andrea and I needed to hear this. We had used the word "stagnant" in a conversation at the coffee shop the day before. We were going through one of those times when it felt like there was nothing going on; no new revelations or synchronicities; no new abilities or exciting events. This was the first indication that there were things going on all the time—even if we weren't privy to the plan.

We were also reminded to reach out to our husbands:

"Support your mates for they are all struggling to reach new heights,
and therefore they are meeting their own challenges head on."

Spirit reminded us that our husbands were with us on this spiritual journey as well, and needed our support.

Crazy Together

There were times when we felt like we were going crazy. Just the fact that we were sitting around talking to Spirit, or receiving messages felt crazy at times. It helped us to know that we *probably* were not crazy, just because there were two other people we trusted who were getting the same information, and having the same weird experiences.

Emotional support was very important, whether it was in relation to wanting things to happen more quickly, or the fluctuations of our moods. We were always there for one another. We reminded each other of the bigger picture, so we would not get bogged down. We helped pull each other out of the current distress by reminding each other: "Remember how, in the past, we were always supported? Well, we're going to be supported through this rough time as well."

Total Trust

Spiritual friends are some of the closest friends that you will ever have. You can say anything without fear of it being used against you; they will only use that information to help you to grow. They won't judge you and they won't talk behind your back. If your story is shared with someone else, it is only to gather help for you, or to assist someone else in getting through a similar crisis.

Issues came up within the group that we didn't want others to know about us, but they came up specifically because they needed healing. For me, they were related to body image and guilt and fear from past life experiences. These issues needed to be exposed, so they could be healed and released.

One friend was able to raise the issue of a long-hidden sexual abuse that occurred with someone she knew. She couldn't share this with me until she knew I wouldn't judge her—or the assailant. Once the information was brought in to the open, she was able to release it.

Spiritual friends are important because odd things will happen to you. You may have experiences with energy, and ghosts (see chapter 15), and past lives, or your divine life mission. Others don't always understand your experiences and aren't always ready to hear what's happening.

For example, when I began to feel Spirit touching me at night, while meditating, or when I saw an Angelic presence before me in the form of a block of color, I initially told no one other than Frank, Andrea and Julie, because I thought other people would think I was nuts. Believe me, even though I was *very* excited, I didn't run out of my office shouting, "Hey, I just saw a green Angel energy next to Harvey, and I'm pretty sure it was Archangel Raphael!" No, instead, I just screamed with delight inside my head until I could call Andrea or Julie.

It was the same when I began to see colors in the auras around people. I wanted to stop them in mid-sentence and say, "Did you know there is the most beautiful blue around you?"

But I knew I would lose credibility. With spiritual friends, you can tell them all the crazy things that are happening to you, and they'll just be happy for you. They'll help you push forward and learn and follow your divine life mission. They will help you stay on track more consistently, and follow your heart.

Please use discernment in your friendships. You may be operating from the principles of trust, love, respect and confidentiality, but they may not. Tread lightly until you know if they have your best interests at heart, so that you don't inadvertently give your power away by misplacing your trust.

Finding Like-Minded Friends

When you find spiritual friends, they should give you spiritual responses in all situations. Instead of taking sides and saying, "You're right; he's a jerk!" they're more inclined to say something like, "I can see how it feels to you, but now tell me his perspective." They'll help pull you back on track instead of letting you get sucked into the anger.

Instead of saying, "Oh my God! You are in such financial trouble, what are you going to do?" they'll say something like, "Keep the faith. It will work out. Remember the last time you were in a similar situation and everything was provided? It will be the same this time if you just remain positive and look for opportunities."

Instead of saying, "It stinks that you didn't get the job," your friend will remind you, "I'll bet Spirit knows there's an even better job for you. Be patient and it will show up."

These friends keep you on track, so you don't get pulled into moments of disappointment. They remind you that your prayers will be answered. When you say, "It's never going to happen," your friends might say, "Be patient and give Spirit some time to line it up for you. Remember that things don't happen overnight." These words are not just meaningless platitudes; they are truths. They help keep you aligned with higher spiritual concepts.

Remember to help each other and to keep like-minded people close by. Find them by sharing your beliefs with others, attending workshops and visiting metaphysical bookstores for starters. At the same time, reach out to people who are *not* like-minded and help them along their journey as well.

Complementary Messages

Another way we support each other is through the messages we receive. For our trinity, they were often in the form of parallel messages. Two or more of us would receive the same guidance at the same time. That gave us confirmation that we really were getting the information from a higher source. Without this confirmation, I would have dismissed everything I received as just my ego talking.

There were times when all kinds of things between the three of us lined up. Sometimes the messages received during meditation would be the same or complementary. What we experienced during meditation, like head rocking and Spirit touches, also happened at the same general time. There was a point when Andrea and I both received the message at the same time to be clearing our chakras. We realized somewhere in the middle of it that we were both doing it. Andrea's path and mine became so similar that when one experienced something and the other became discouraged because she had not experienced it yet, we would just remind each other that the other one would probably have the same experience within two weeks.

Often, even our dreams were the same. One night, Andrea and I both had a dream about Egypt. On another night, Andrea and Tracy dreamed about Jesus. I suspect this was to let us know that we shared lives together in those times. Perhaps we even traveled out-of-body to those dimensions while we slept.

Sometimes similar things would occur in our lives. On a trip to Manhattan, Andrea and I were visiting a number of shops, trying to find a necklace or bracelet for Julie. Andrea broke a necklace and lost an earring and I had a bracelet fall off. Andrea felt strongly that there was a reason behind it.

When we returned home, we raised the issue with Julie, and she said that she was also having jewelry fall off her body, and it was happening at an increased rate. Then she was told that jewelry actually interferes with your power and was told not to wear it, especially jewelry that totally encircles parts of the body, like bracelets and necklaces. She was told that items made of substances like string or leather were better than those made of metal.

None of us liked this message about jewelry and we all continue to wear it! We are still in physical form and want to enjoy life's pleasures! But I wear less jewelry and when I do wear it, I try to wear pieces that don't totally encircle parts of the body, like cuff bracelets and post earrings. (By the way, we ended up getting Julie a candle!)

This One's for You

One of my messages came through Bonnie's husband, Anthony. He made sure that Bonnie gave me the message to "Trust my vibes."

That was very meaningful for me, because at that time I was getting a strong message to write this book, but I was full of self-doubts about my abilities and qualifications, and I was fearful that Spirit wouldn't be there to help me (even though I knew better!). Very shortly after receiving Anthony's message, I began to write this book. The message from Anthony was so important because it gave confirmation to the guidance I'd been receiving.

There were many exciting times when each of us contributed information to the same story—like when Andrea was trying to find out who her spirit guides were. In meditation, she learned that one guide's name was Horatio. I was skeptical about this because I never heard of an Angel or Biblical figure named Horatio. I searched my Angel book for an Angel named Horatio, but there wasn't one.

I felt guided to search the internet and found a reference to Horatio Nelson. There was a beautiful spiritual poem written by Nelson and I believed he was her guide. Then Julie saw the name "Rhodes" in a vision, and she knew that it was Horatio Rhodes. I was disappointed because Andrea and Julie got their information through divine inspiration, while I was stumbling around doing mundane internet searches.

I realize now that I was actually being guided to those sources. I did another search on Horatio Rhodes and found a write-up on Horatio Rhodes Nelson! It was the same person! My faith in myself was restored. When I showed Julie a printout, she remarked that she had seen that same odd font in her vision. These experiences helped support the idea that we are all connected, and we are much more effective when we work together than apart.

Support Each Other

Physically we helped each other with pain issues by sending healing energy and doing hands-on healing sessions. While I was working so hard to resolve my knee pain, and not succeeding very well, Julie was told to step in and "take it" from me. On an ego level, her stepping in was upsetting to me because it seemed to indicate that I couldn't heal myself. But we were told that she was a complement to what I was already doing. That felt a little better!

The three of us had been physically separated for several weeks because of sicknesses and family commitments. As we sat at my kitchen table, Julie was shown that we were joined together energetically. When I asked why, she was told, "synergy." Synergy is a coming together of energies. "You are joining together energetically, so that if there comes a time when you are separated physically, you will still know if one of you is in trouble and needs support. A portal has been created."

A few weeks later, I received some bad news and was extremely sad. I wasn't ready to call anyone, but I did need to talk, so I imagined an energetic portal and screamed into it, "Help me!" Within a couple hours Julie called to check in. A few weeks later, I "happened" to call Julie as she was on the way to the emergency room with her daughter. This portal thing sure was convenient!

It's important to find people who can support you and whom you can support. These should be mutually beneficial relationships. During difficult times, allow yourself to lean more heavily on others for support, but when that time has passed, it's better to back off and stand on your own again.

Initially, Julie was a major support to Andrea and me, but as we gained knowledge, confidence, intuition and ability, we were able to strike more of a balance and offer support to her as well. It felt empowering to lend her support, so please don't feel like you cannot allow the tables to turn and be supported by others. You'll be denying them a beautiful gift. I'm feeling the balance turning in the relationship with my dear friend, Tracy, as she, too, gains in knowledge, confidence and intuitive ability. In the early days, she thought she was leaning too heavily on me, as she struggled through a divorce and began exploring her spirituality. But she was providing me with opportunities to speak my truth, refine my thinking and operate from love.

Share with Your Mate

Trust that your significant other was put in your life for a reason. If you are in a relationship, share as much of your experiences as you can. If you find that you can't share everything, share the absolute most that he or she can tolerate. This spiritual being is who you are; not sharing this part of you will make you feel as if you are withholding your truth.

I share everything with Frank and it has been such a blessing. He doesn't always understand what's going on, and he has not yet experienced all the things I have (although he has had other experiences that I have not), but he's always supportive, and I enjoy sharing with him.

I'm aware that many people have significant others who are threatened by their experiences and beliefs. At times, our husbands felt threatened when they felt we were moving faster than they were and that we might be moving away from them. I'd back off a bit and just discuss day-to-day things when I sensed it was too much for Frank. I told him everything, but not necessarily on the day it occurred. I tended to wait for the crazier stuff to play out so I'd have the full picture, which might not appear quite as crazy (especially when later events confirmed the guidance).

I think it's similar with parents and friends, except that, in a sense, there is less need to share all the details. My parents knew little about all this until I realized I was going to write a book and felt it was time to start sharing! I began by sharing pieces they would be more likely to relate to.

As for friends, many people in my life know very little about my spiritual experiences, because I've not had a reason to share. As I've said, my close friends know everything and I'm very lucky to have them.

If you need to be talking to everyone about your spirituality all the time, I'd recommend you sit quietly with that. See if it is coming as a calling from your highest source. If not, see if it is coming from a need to be recognized or a need to feel special. If it is, work on getting to the bottom of that and healing it.

Teach the Children Well

Children are another story. These souls are also put in our lives for a reason. I think we have an obligation to share our own discoveries and spiritual beliefs with our children, and to help them discover their own truths. It's especially important now, because humanity is in a major transition, and the children are the ones who will move us to the next step.

With very young children, it's easy for them to join us in our discoveries. For older children, it can be more challenging—unless they have "clairs" of their own. Then it can be a great relief to them to learn that they are not so "weird" after all!

I struggled with presenting some of my beliefs to my kids. By the time I became spiritually awakened, they were old enough to have been influenced by society. I shared slowly. Sometimes they'd roll their eyes and give each other that "there she goes again" look. But later, I'd get follow-up questions, and soon they began relating their own experiences.

I was worried because even though *I* knew what to discuss and when, I was less sure about them. They were eight and ten when they had their first Reiki attunements and we had lots of talks at that point. We talked about the fact that they had to tread lightly, yet they had to be who they were. So far, so good. They have both had some fun interactions with their friends by showing them how to feel energy with their hands. I've been pleased to see that they do know how much they can share and with whom.

The Religions
Church (or any religious affiliation) is yet another story. What do you do when your beliefs and experiences come into conflict with your church, or your minister is openly hostile about your belief in past lives, or laying-on-of-hands, and your religious participation becomes a source of angst instead of support? There seem to be only two choices: stay or leave.

My friend, Terry, is a funny, passionate healer and a devout Catholic. She *loves* the Catholic Church and is extremely involved in it. Terry can see Angelic energy; she can feel the energy in the room and around people's bodies. She can tell you what is wrong with you just by looking at you. Terry has elected to stay in the church, even though she doesn't always fit in, because it works for her. She gets great comfort from her religion. She does not feel constrained by it. She feels she can be a positive influence within her church.

Others have chosen to leave their religion of origin. Typically it is because they feel constrained or they feel the church would not approve of their new beliefs. Many feel incredible guilt because they were taught that not attending church is a sin.

Others have found different churches or places of worship that are more open-minded, where there is plenty of space for their new beliefs. In fact, many ministers, priests and Rabbis have become Reiki-attuned, or exposed to new ideas, and some have had unusual experiences that they wish that they could share with their congregations—and some have!

I chose to leave my church after returning for two years. I didn't agree with what my children were being taught. There was too much emphasis placed on fear of God versus love of God, and they were told not to even date someone who was not Christian, because there was no chance they could marry. I wanted something more expansive for them.

I think the constraints that some are feeling are the result of the *exoteric* teachings of the religion, and not the *esoteric*. The exoteric teachings are the *outward* teachings of each religion that are deemed fit for the masses—what we learn at church, in the synagogue, mosque, etc. The esoteric teachings were reserved for initiates; those who had special interest and understanding of the underlying truths. Jesus taught one thing to the crowds and another to his disciples, because they could handle more.

The experiences I describe in this book are akin to the esoteric teachings. I believe that the esoteric teachings of all the religions—what *truly* underpins them—are similar. So the outer trappings of your religion might feel constraining, but as you awaken and experience the spiritual phenomena described in this book, you are actually aligning with the *true* foundations of all the religions.

Calling All Angels

Pay attention to where you are being guided and to whom you are being guided. If you feel a strong impulse to reach out to someone, you will likely find them being surprisingly responsive and open to your words.

Remember to ask for support from Spirit and ask Spirit to send you friends with whom you can share mutual support. I call on Spirit constantly. I call on them in times of sadness, to be with me and comfort me. I call in Angels or Jesus (and sometimes all of them) and just sit quietly while their vibrations support me. Other times, in anger, I yell at them to help me.

Asking for Help and Support

Sometimes I feel a strong need to talk to Will Linville, especially when I need confirmation, or when I'm feeling emotionally distressed. It was helpful for me to talk to him when Spirit would not talk to me through Julie, even though it felt like I was cheating! On the other hand, sometimes

I just need to trust the way things are playing out, without getting "insider information" from Will.

You don't have to have someone like Will or Julie, but it can make life a whole lot easier! Spiritual mentors who are further down the path can help let you know what's coming, validate your experiences and point out when you are in your ego or your fear. Be careful not to equate psychic ability with advanced spirituality. Even though they have a psychic talent, they may still be operating from a low vibration.

If you do feel the need to find someone with a clearer connection, be careful not to lean on them too much, at the expense of developing your own abilities. Don't take what they say as gospel (if you do, you'll be giving away your power), but instead measure the accuracy of what they say by how well it fits with your own guidance. Check in with your body as well as your mind and spirit. If their advice makes you feel tense and anxious, it probably isn't right for you (unless it calls for some degree of change that intimidates you). Sometimes we need to respect our own perceived limitations and sometimes we need to push beyond them.

Know also that the information that someone with a clear connection gives you is based on what is being presented *in that moment*. The future can change, based on your choices and the choices of others. If you don't like what you're being told about the future, try to change it. You have free will and you can make different choices.

Chapter 14

Jesus

A Loving Role Model

This is the chapter that almost wasn't. The very first night that I sat with my notes, to see if I could begin to see the book inside, I was awed by what happened. As I read through the journal, individual chapters became readily apparent from what I had considered random, chronological occurrences. As I encountered each new one, I wrote a topic at the top of the page and wrote a summary under it. One of those headings was "Jesus." I referred to those pages as "The Jesus Pages."

I really didn't know what to do with them. They contained accounts of numerous visits from him and lots of wisdom that he gave us. Quite honestly, although I had become comfortable with Jesus visiting, and I loved the feel of his energy, I was afraid to talk about him with anyone outside our inner circle.

In our society and the larger world, we have come to think of Jesus as someone on a pedestal to be revered. For many, he is synonymous with God. He is not thought of as human, and certainly not someone you could have a conversation with.

I never had an understanding of Jesus until I hit thirty-nine, when Julie began telling me about her conversations with him and I began to have my own encounters with his energy. I knew who Jesus was in the Bible, but he didn't make sense to me. I could never really get my head around the concept.

Heck, for years after my car accident, I discounted the concept of God, so Jesus didn't stand a chance with me! It wasn't until my first Reiki attunement, when I felt heat in my hands, that I knew God existed. Even after I understood unequivocally that God existed, I still couldn't comprehend Jesus.

One night I was trying to figure out if Jesus was real or just another nice parable. So I threw it out to God. I said, "Okay, I get *You* now. But I don't know about Jesus. I need You to tell me if Jesus was real or not."

I said it just like that. I always talked to God like that. I figured He knew all the other stuff I was saying and thinking, so there was no need to pretty it up.

The next day I felt inspired to open my copy of *A Course in Miracles,*[1] a book which is reputed to be channeled from Jesus. I've owned this book for awhile, but never felt drawn to read it. As I read, I knew I was hearing his voice and I never doubted again. Of course, once Jesus began visiting us, there was no turning back.

As I mentioned earlier, Jesus told us in the Bible that we can do all that he did and more: "Truly, truly I say to you, he who believes in me will also do the works that I do; and greater works than these he will do."[2] I believe we disrespect him when we don't believe his words. I respect and admire the way Jesus stepped fully into his abilities, and then had the guts to speak his truth, especially given the viciousness of the world he lived in. He was showing us mastery—how to be *all* you are capable of *as a human being.* When we raise Jesus to the status of a God, we disrespect his message. He wanted to be an example to us; to show us what we are capable of doing and being.

It was not only Jesus who performed healings; he told his disciples to "Heal the sick."[3] And then he said, "He that receiveth you receiveth me, and he that receiveth me receiveth him that sent me."[4]

The ability to heal this way comes from God, and it is meant to be shared with many—not just limited to Jesus. But for Christians, Jesus is the inspiration: "The disciple is not above his master . . . it is enough for the disciple that he be as his master."[5] The Avatars of other religions were showing different cultures the same thing.

The Reminder

I put The Jesus Pages aside for a long time. They didn't make it into the first draft—or the second, for that matter. I put them away, thinking that maybe they would go into a different book. Then I felt like I hit a wall. The book sat for months. I went to a lecture series that Will gave in Las Vegas, on energy work. Tracy came with me and we had a blast enjoying the sights and sounds of Vegas.

Will doesn't use notes when he speaks; he simply goes with "what presents." On the second day, he came up behind us after a break and said, "We're going to be talking about Yeshua ben Joseph (Jesus) next, because this is what you're presenting with. Feel free to ask any questions." Will presented the whole next part of his talk on Jesus and I had no question other than, "What am I supposed to ask?"

So I didn't ask anything.

We took a lunch break and Will came up behind us again and said, "We're going to be finishing up with our dear friend, Yeshua, so be sure to ask any question that you have—any question." Clearly I was missing something. I sat listening to the next segment, thinking hard about what Will was saying and what I needed to ask. Tears began welling up in my eyes. I couldn't remember lots of the specifics, but I saw myself in the scenes that Will described with Jesus and I felt the intensity of my love for Jesus and a sadness about how things unfolded at the time of the crucifixion.

At that point, I immediately knew that The Jesus Pages were supposed to be included in this book. In my head, on continuous loop, I heard, "Oh, no. God, no, no, no. I can't do that. I'm not ready." The room was spinning.

The fear of persecution came flooding back. I fought it for a few moments and then tentatively raised my hand to confirm my knowing with Will. At that point, he took every remaining question *but* mine and quickly wrapped up the discussion. In hindsight, I know that he knew that I had finally gotten it—there was no need to address it publicly. I also needed to sit with the thought on my own for a while, and work out my issues with it.

Will then moved on to a meditation, to show us how to access the Akashic Records. This is an etheric realm that holds all the knowledge and events of the Universe. Will led us through the meditation and eventually had us see a door, open the door, see a library and pull down a book. I did what he said and held my book.

"Look at the title of the book," Will said.

I saw "The Story."

"The story of what?" I asked.

I looked again: "The Story of Jesus."

Needless to say, the soundtrack went off in my head again: "Oh, no. God, no, no, no. I can't do that. I'm not ready." The room started spinning again.

By the time I saw Will for a private session the next day, I had calmed down. I reminded myself that if writing about Jesus was something that I incarnated here to do, then I would do it. The fear diminished. Will confirmed all that I knew to be true, and told me that I would channel what was needed.

But why include Jesus here at all? This is a book about our potential as humans, our next evolutionary step—not our past. But remember that there is no past or future. Jesus bleeds through to this lifetime for so many of us because his message of love and self-mastery is timeless and all-important. His words were simple and brilliant. But much has been lost. We need to go back and see the simple message and bring it into our lives. We also need to be reminded to stop following him. Do what he did, yes. Bring that essence into our own lives, yes. Use him as a role model for our own behavior, yes. But don't blindly follow him. Don't follow anyone.

Jesus Visits

Julie had been speaking with her guides since she was eighteen. They advised her on all kinds of topics, including mundane, day-to-day events. Andrea and I meditated nightly, because we felt energy more keenly in the quiet of the night and were eager to establish the kind of connection with Spirit that Julie had. She, however, meditated infrequently at night, though her guides reminded her that she needed to be meditating more so she could move more quickly in her life purpose. So she began, rather reluctantly, to meditate more often.

One morning, she came to yoga very excited, because Jesus had visited her during the night. She said his energy was overwhelming and very exciting. The next few nights he didn't visit, and Julie longed to feel his healing vibration again. She'd coyly ask whoever came that night if Jesus could come again and they'd laugh at her. (Apparently they think we are quite funny and laugh at us a lot. We ask a lot of stupid questions because the veil blocks us from accessing information that we already know when we're on the Other Side.)

After that, Jesus began visiting Julie fairly regularly during meditation. All of us began receiving various signs that we had been present during the time that Jesus was in physical form on Earth. I began having lots of discomfort in my shoulders and shortness of breath. I felt like I needed to take deep breaths, but couldn't quite do it. My thoughts kept returning to the time of the crucifixion. Finally, I recognized that I had been there at the time of the crucifixion. Julie confirmed my suspicions and told me that my name had been Rebekah. At that point, the discomfort and shortness of breath disappeared and never returned.

Confirmation

As I've said, I typically recognize which entity is with me by their vibration. I identified Ariel and Michael, but then a new vibration presented and I couldn't figure out who it was. Soon after, I attended a workshop on spirit guides. It was a small, interactive group. During the meditation, the facilitator asked us to quietly say what we were experiencing. I told her that I heard a tone in my ear. She said, "That's because Spirit just showed up all around us."

I said, "Now I feel a vibration on my face and arms." It was a very fine, sweet vibration.

She said, "That's Jesus. He's just come over to you." She was watching while we all sat with our eyes closed, trying to maximize our ability to perceive with our other senses. Every once in a while, I'd sneak a peek, but I couldn't see anyone. I was thrilled just to feel Spirit around me. The other attendees made comments and either knew who was around them or were told by the instructor. Then all the guides proceeded to do energy work on us.

So now I knew who my new vibration was. It was Jesus. What a cool introduction! From there my ability to perceive him grew, and I learned that I could ask him to come and he would. (It's no surprise that I did that frequently for a while!)

Now, in times of stress or perceived difficulty, I often hear a voice in my head that says, "In this world, not of it," that repeats over and over until I acknowledge it. I believe it is a reminder from Jesus to walk through this world as an observer and not to let yourself be pulled into the fear, worry, grief and anger. To paraphrase in my own words: Know that the events are beautiful and don't let the crap get stuck on you!

"In this world, not of it" is an incredibly simple but important message. If you are feeling stress, anger, or sadness from the circumstances in your life, you are not heeding his message. It's important for us to walk through circumstances as much as possible, without being affected by them, or else we will need to heal from that stress. We need to fully get that emotion out of our energy fields and our bodies. Think of it as getting more stuff stuck on you (new hurts) at the same time that you're trying to get the old stuff off. You're slowing your progress by creating more healing to do. And you're not fully walking forward in faith that God's got your back, and everything on your path is part of His plan.

Where Are We Going?

Slowing your progress to where? To Christ Consciousness or God Consciousness. Christ Consciousness does not refer to Jesus Christ, though he was *one* of the Avatars who attained Christ Consciousness. This is when you become part of All and Everything—you transcend your ego and move beyond petty wants and needs. You recognize that all that is around you is perfect because God created it and God is perfect. You understand that all can be used for God's purpose. You've surrendered yourself to God's will and given yourself over to His service.

Julie shared this very powerful thought. She said, "Christ Consciousness is realizing that even your 'mistakes' are not your own. God will use them as well." In that sense, they weren't mistakes. You just do the best you can, and then you don't take credit or blame for *anything*. It is a very high vibrational state.

Achieving Christ Consciousness is important for each of us because any movement in that direction helps to uplift the consciousness of the world. Deepak Chopra explains Christ Consciousness and how to achieve it in *The Third Jesus: The Christ We Cannot Ignore.*[6] The first Jesus is the historical figure, the second is the theological one and the third is Christ Consciousness, the one Jesus was really encouraging us to embody.

I love Chopra's book. *The Third Jesus* explained much of what I was feeling and experiencing and helped to clarify statements in Scripture that were confusing for me.

A Simple Life

When I held Jesus out as someone too special, he laughed and said to Julie, "Tell her I was not special. I was just a man."

That took some readjusting. It's because of that exchange that I decided not to capitalize "him" and "he" when referring to Jesus or the other great Avatars. I don't think they'd approve of being referred to differently than anyone else.

As I worked on channeling the information that Jesus wanted to share about his life, I became frustrated with my ability to receive only a few sentences about each topic. I assumed there was more to come. But in a conversation with Julie, Jesus showed up to discuss the book, and he kept repeating, "The story of my life is simple. It was a simple life." He seems to want the record set straight without making it all about him again. Different versions of his story are coming out now through many writers—there are many new books about him. Many writings of his time are now coming to light as we see in the discoveries of the Nag Hammadi Library and the Dead Sea Scrolls. More ancient writings will be found in the future.

So let's turn to this simple life. The following is a blend of information I received from Will and directly from my own guidance during meditation and while writing.

Jesus came from a family of means. They chose, however, to live simply and not get caught up in things of this world. He had gems and jewels that were a great source of enjoyment for him—they were a great passion. He was able to use them to assist him in manipulating the elements. Many people today are able to feel the vibratory patterns of crystals and gemstones and use them to assist in healing, manifesting and connecting with other realms.

His early life was spent in intense education, preparing him for his future role.

John baptized Jesus with water. The water was symbolic of purification. He was purifying himself from the elements of fire, rain, water and air to show mankind that this world is an illusion; to show man that, "You need not carry all of these elements through your physical." For me, this was once again a reminder to be "in this world, not of it." He was symbolically showing mankind that he was not going to be controlled by his egoic structure. Jesus did not want man to be corrupted by earthly ways and drawn off track from the Father.

The story of the loaves and the fishes took place at Jesus' wedding to Mary Magdalene. He had known her for years as he grew up with her and both were educated in the ways of the Essenes. The Essenes were often referred to as a sect of Judaism, but their beliefs went well beyond Judaism. The Essenes incorporated beliefs from Egypt, Persia, Greece and elsewhere.

Jesus multiplied the bread and the fish so that there was enough for all attending the celebration. Through the bread and the fish, Jesus showed people the abundance that is all around them.

There is truly enough for everyone. He desired to show them their own ability to manifest what they need. He was playing with the elements, going beyond what was locked in as a reality into what truly is.

The miracles that he created—walking on water, healing the sick, raising the dead, creating abundance—were not miracles; they were examples of what man is truly capable of when he steps fully into his potential. This is what we are supposed to remember when we remember him—our own capability.

Jesus' message and life were all about love and he wanted us to know that we are all capable of great love. When I asked what he wanted us to know about him, I heard: "The love. It all goes back to the love. Be the love. Live the love." Jesus treated everyone with love because he saw the beauty in everyone—their God Consciousness. He knew that everyone was capable of making choices that could instantly change their vibration.

Jesus was aware that he was to be crucified. It could not have happened without his consent on some level. He knew it was his destiny. He did not, however, die on the cross. Instead, he allowed himself to be crucified to conquer the fear of death. It was his last remaining obstacle. He faced it for himself and for mankind.

For himself, he showed that he was able to take himself to a near death state by exercising control over all bodily functions as he was trained to do when he was younger. He showed himself that he could face the fear of death and return to the world of the living. For mankind, he showed that our biggest fear—death—was meaningless because we are eternal beings who pass from this world of the physical and "rise" back to the world of the energetic and spiritual, despite the most horrific cause of death.

What If?

Wow. That last part threw me. I felt lied to and cheated somehow. I was angry and confused. "Why is this even important?" I thought. "Why tell us now?" A part of me said, "Go away! Leave me alone! Go tell someone else."

These new ideas were presented as absolutes, like "This is the way it was." Period. But over time, I've come to realize they were meant as "What ifs." What if Jesus was rich? What if he married Mary Magdalene? What if he lived and didn't die on the cross? What does it change? Anything? Everything? Nothing?

I believe the reason for presenting these ideas was to get us to question *everything*. Get us to consider that some of what we are being taught is untrue or a misinterpretation or a parable or . . . maybe it *is* true. The point is to question it. Sit with it. Meditate on it. Because you *will* be shown. Make your beliefs your own.

We all have the power—inside and outside of churches, synagogues, mosques, etc.—to know the truth. These are called mystical experiences— having knowledge revealed from within. We are all capable of being mystics. It's also called gnosis, a knowing from within. The push from Spirit was to figure out what we believe for ourselves. Personally, I love to use many of the ancient spiritual texts, like the Bible, the Bhagavad Gita, and Kaballistic writings, to guide my questioning.

Without the initial jolt to my beliefs, turning them upside down, I might not have done so much soul-searching to learn what was true for me. It was important for me that the key event of the crucifixion be called into question, to get my attention. If I could question such key events, I could question *any* of my beliefs and begin to wonder whether there was something different or deeper to my interpretations of events and Scripture.

So what do I believe now? It's really not important what I think. It's much more important what *you* think and what *you* are shown as a result of your questioning.

I'll tell you that some of my thinking changed. And I expanded my questions well beyond these few Biblical incidents.

Let's look at what it would mean if we accepted that Jesus' life was simple and he was a *model* to follow, not a *leader*.

- Would Jesus still be the son of God? Yes, we all are.
- Was Jesus sent by God to be a model for living? Yes, he showed us how to achieve self-mastery, including unconditional love. He showed us all this and more is possible and gave us a blueprint. Using this blueprint, you, too, might serve as a model for others.
- Did he rise from the dead? Yes, he rose into what some call his light body, the ethereal image described in the Bible. He either did it after dying on the cross; or after coming down alive from the cross, having achieved a higher vibration. But the bottom line probably remains the same.
- Is he alive today? Yes, we are all eternal.
- Did he die for our sins? Yes, symbolically if you believe he didn't die on the cross and literally if you believe he did. But on the other hand, this begs the question of sin versus karma.

Sin vs. Karma

The concept of sin, which is an incredible instructional tool to keep us on the correct path, may not operate the way we typically think. Consider instead, the Eastern concept of karma. Man is free to make any choices. We are born with free will. However, there *are* consequences for our decisions. Of course, there are the obvious manmade consequences in the form of our laws, and punishment for disobedience to those laws. But there are spiritual consequences as well, and that may be where the concept of sin came from in the first place.

If you choose a low vibrational act, it will put you into a lower vibrational frequency, and events of a lower nature will be attracted to your energy field. Consider how you feel when you lie. You typically feel badly. You are wracked with guilt and can't seem to let it go. Even if you rationalize the lie to yourself, it still sits there, eating at you. That's part of the meaning of the Biblical saying, "The Truth shall set you free." It feels better to tell the truth because the vibration of that choice is higher. A larger meaning of the saying is that once you understand the Truth of God and eternal life, you are freed from all that holds you captive in this world.

How do you know the vibration of an act? In two ways. First you feel the vibration associated with your behavior. Think about how you feel when you are angry with someone for hurting you. You feel awful. Anger is a low vibrational feeling. Now consider how you feel when you forgive. You instantly feel better, lighter. That's because you made a higher vibrational decision. Your mind does not constantly return to the hurt and touch that bruise, because you've let it go. You don't keep that person tied to you through the energy of your anger.

Think about how it feels when you are depressed. You feel so heavy that you don't even want to get out of bed. You have a hard time moving. Now think about something happy and you feel instantly lighter.

Acts that society deems "bad," like murder and stealing, have their own vibrations. This is true even when the person committing the act is incapable of perceiving the vibration—as in the case of the sociopath or psychopath. There is still a vibrational consequence.

Another way to know the vibration of an act or feeling is to read *Power Versus Force*[7] by David Hawkins. He calibrates different human behaviors and emotions. Using the book, you can confirm what your being already knows about vibrational choices.

Saying that there is no sin is not a Get Out of Jail Free card. There are still karmic consequences for your behavior. Jesus used the cross scenario to show you that you are an eternal being, free from death and sin.

Why Not Buddha?
Some might ask why I included a chapter on Jesus, and not on Buddha, or the other great Avatars. Jesus is the Avatar energy that I feel most connected with. I believe in all the Avatars. They each have an energy that can be of assistance to those who call on them. Each Avatar came at a different time to appeal to a different culture and geographic region, but they all had similar messages. Each person can choose the one they identify with and call on that energy for assistance. I believe that it is important for each of us, though, to approach all of the Avatars' teachings with a Gnostic attitude of "Show me what is true." Consider for the moment that there are no absolute truths and see where that leads you.

Chapter 15

Ghosts

Who's There?

Julie told me many stories about her encounters with ghosts. Ghosts are the spirits of people who have died but have not made a full transition to the Other Side. They are not Angels or spirit guides. She told me stories about how they'd show up around her son, Carlo. She didn't see them, but she felt their distinct energies and conversed with them.

He was aware of them on some level, and he was often frightened by them at night. He would get scared and Julie would go in and shoo them away. She was never frightened by them. "Simply tell them to go and they have to go," she'd tell him. Her attitude was that yes, they were there and that was a part of life.

One night Carlo came in very upset because there were ghosts all around him. She saw them and was very angry they were bothering him. She went through every room, chasing them out of the house and telling them to go. Another night, they bothered her all night as she tried to sleep. As each one showed up, she would send it to the Light to help it pass completely. She said she felt like a cashier at a grocery check-out. As she told one to go to the Light, another one would show up. Half asleep, she finally asked Spirit what was going on. Spirit said, "Just send them to the Light." So that was how she spent her night. With his mom on duty, Carlo now sleeps peacefully!

Joy Gardner had a similar experience in Sedona, where she encountered hundreds of Navajo Spirits of the dead who seemed to be trapped there. She just opened a portal, and they all went through and into the Light.

She experienced a similar phenomenon after the 2011 earthquake/tsunami in Japan, when so many people died. She had a sense of standing next to a passageway and holding open a curtain, as a long line of people passed through, into the Light. The hardest part for her was that each person insisted on bowing to her before passing (and of course it would be rude not to bow back). So then she asked her late husband to come and help her hold open the other side of the curtain, thinking that would make the line go faster. Then each person had to bow to each of them!

The Sitting Room

When we moved into a new house there was something creepy about the sitting room that was off the master bedroom. I had a sense of a presence there. That was all; nothing concrete. I then began to have experiences where the door to the sitting room would blow open. (This was even before the door-opening events that I described earlier.) Some days there was wind outside and some days there wasn't. That wasn't the cause. It added to the creepiness of the sitting room. Let me just say that I *never, ever* felt a presence of any kind before then. Never.

I continued to have these experiences where the door would blow open and I would feel uneasy and I'd feel a presence. I called Will and asked him whether there was someone there. He immediately stopped and I heard him saying something that was too fast for me to comprehend, but I realized that he was talking to the ghost. When he was done, he said to me, "Do you remember how to bind an entity to the sun?"

I loved the way he did that. He always spoke to you as if you had all the knowledge in the world and you had simply forgotten it. I wanted to say, "Are you freaking kidding me?! I've never encountered a spirit before, let alone bound it to the sun!" But I simply said, "No."

He said, "What you have to do when you recognize that someone who has passed is there is to bind them to the Light. They have not found their way yet." You actually say out loud, "I bind you to the sun." I did what he said, and after that, I didn't feel the presence anymore and the door did not blow open. For a while.

Find a Better Light

Then it began to happen again. I thought, "But Will told me that once you bound an entity to the sun it has to go."

Julie and Andrea came over and I asked them to come up into the sitting room. "Can you feel anything?" I asked, without explaining what Will told me or what I felt. Julie picked up that there was a man and a woman. She could communicate with them, and she learned that the man had passed in a car accident and didn't realize he had died because it happened so quickly. When the woman passed, she saw the man and became confused about where to go. She told me that they were afraid and they had been attracted to my light. They thought that *I* was *the* Light they were heading for.

I found this absolutely hysterical. I was immediately reminded of the *Men in Black*[1] movie where Tommy Lee Jones, as agent K, opens up the locker that has little tiny aliens in it and when they see him they say, "All hail K, all hail K," and they worship his light—which is really his glow-in-the-dark watch.

According to Will, as my light grew, it was more attractive to spirits who were stuck, not knowing where to go. As it happens, my department at work was housed in the same building as a nursing home, and many people died in that building—often after long illnesses and heavy sedation, so they didn't always realize they had passed.

So according to Will, they were following me home. He said I needed to clear myself of them before I left work. I needed to tell them they were not welcome to stay and that there was another Light they should find and follow. I would always add that "Jesus will take you by the hand and lead you to the Light if you cannot find it on your own."

Then I thought maybe I was overtaxing Jesus or giving him a job that really was not His, so I began to say "Jesus or someone he designates will take you to the Light!" Each time, the ghost would then be gone. Since then I've learned that it is not taxing Jesus, so don't worry!

I never shared any of this with the kids because I thought it would scare them. But my son, Eric, would not sit in the sitting room alone. He would go in there if other people were there, but he would leave the room as soon as they left.

Ghosts continued to come, so whenever I realized they were there, I would just bind them to the sun and they left. More recently, the feeling of the sitting room has become completely different, because it is filled with Angelic presences who are here to support the book. Eric came into the room the other day and said, "I like this room. It feels good now."

Turn Off the Light
There's an antique light next to Frank's side of the bed that clicks on-and-off when you roll the switch between your fingers. One night, in the middle of the night, I heard "click, click." The light went on-and-off. I heard "click" and the light went on again and stayed on. I said, "Frank." No answer. I said it again louder. No answer. "Frank! Do you really need that light on?" I shook him, feeling irritated that he would turn the light on in the middle of the night. I startled him awake. He had been out cold and had not even realized the light was on.

I guess I'd been learning from Julie's stories, because I just turned to the thin air and declared, "That is *not* okay! You may not come here in the middle of the night and turn lights on! You've scared me and that is not okay! Go now! I bind you to the Light!" I never had that experience again.

I surprised myself by not being afraid. I guess it was because I had heard so many nonchalant, guess-who-showed-up-last-night stories. I also felt no hostile energy from these ghosts. It was as if they just wanted to wake me up to talk. Perhaps they just wanted to get Frank in trouble for turning on the lights!

My daughter, Molly, once told me that she woke up in the middle of the night and found her light on. I asked her what she did and she said she got up and turned it off (Duh, Mom!). I asked her if she was frightened by it and she said she was, but she just climbed back in bed and put her head under the covers. I didn't believe her story at the time. Sorry, Molly.

Another night, at the wall at the foot of the bed, I heard, "BANG, BANG, BANG," moving down the wall. It was as if someone ran along the wall while hitting each of the studs (which, by the way, are covered by sheet-rock). I had the image of the prisoners in the old movies running their tin drinking cups along the cell bars. I told them to stop and bound them to the Light. It stopped.

One night it sounded like there were marbles being dropped on the attic floor above my head. I had no idea what caused the noise because the attic floor is made of rafters and fiberglass. Usually I would not be afraid, but it was so loud and startling that I became afraid. I was lying in bed scared. I thought to bind them to the Light and I did, but I was still afraid.

Then I thought, "I am not alone." I called in Jesus and my guides and I said, "Please comfort me," and I was instantly comforted. A presence surrounded me and I fell back to sleep.

Careful Whom You Call

Andrea's son, Kenny, was meditating one night and he wanted to get into a deeper meditation, so he asked for someone to come and take him deeper. I thought it was such a good, simple idea and wondered why I never thought of it. He then saw a vision that was very disturbing to him. He saw a car accident. There was an ambulance, and the area around the car was roped off. People were moving very slowly and Kenny understood that someone had died in the accident because there was no sense of urgency in the people on the scene. He was frightened by the vision. He didn't know who had been killed.

Andrea called Julie to get more information, and she said, "Listen, you've got to be careful who you call in to assist you. Make sure that it's an Ascended Master or an Angel or a spirit guide, because many entities can step in, but they might have their own agenda." In Kenny's case, the ghost was showing Kenny how he had died.

As your light brightens, you may begin to encounter other entities in your midst. Please DO NOT be afraid. Simply bind them to the Light and tell them to go. They will go. And be careful whom you call in to assist you.

"All hail K."[2]

Conclusion

Or Is This Just The Beginning?

So where is all this heading? I don't know, but it's some of the most fun I have ever had in my life. There are no limits and anything can happen. Frank, Andrea, Tracy and Julie are laughing at me because many of the things that I now state as truths and tips (like be patient while clearing your channel, allow for inaccuracies in intuition, relax and just allow, etc) were things I struggled with as I went along. They saw how impatient and frustrated I was, and how I struggled to figure out the lessons. It's the old case of "Do what I say and not what I did!"

The key point is that *everyone* is capable of gaining access to all the experiences I describe here. It is your birthright. It is your right as a spirit housed in a physical body. You may not believe that you *can* experience all that I describe here, but that's only because you haven't been aware that it was even a choice. It's like having a standard menu without the Daily Specials page. You need only clear your channel. Allow yourself to feel and work with energy. Develop your intuition and invite it to support you in all you do. Ask the Angelic realm to assist you. Focus on what your truth is and speak it. Find that place of love within you and operate from it. Seek support from others and lend yours when needed. Know your power and allow your divine life purpose to present when you're ready for it.

In short, look beyond the veil and remember who you are.

Always be humble as you go through this process. Never think you're better than someone else because you've seemingly figured something out and they haven't. Awakening to spiritual consciousness can come in an instant or it can be a slow process. Never assume that your current truth is *the* truth or the *only* truth.

So where do I go from here? I'll try to be patient and see where life is going. I'm no longer trying to take control. I'll wait to see what I'm being shown. I will seek Spirit's assistance in accomplishing what they show me. I'll experience as much joy along the way as I can and try not to be so serious. I'll attempt to surrender. I'll seek to heal more fully. I'll allow my feelings when the tears and sadness come. When it feels like I'm all alone, I'll remind myself that I'm completely surrounded by Spirit. I'll try to be the best me that I can be.

I am now turning more attention to my body, without sacrificing the mind or spirit. When I was younger, my attention was on mind and body—keeping fit and doing well in school. As I moved into my working years, I focused on my work and taking care of my family and left no time for my body. With my spiritual awakening came excitement and fascination with the spirit that I never even knew existed. The spirit then received all of my attention.

I'm realizing now that the balance of body, mind and spirit is so important. I'm at a point where I have achieved a higher vibration, but to go further, the body has to become fit and strong again. I'm starting to eat whole and raw foods as a way of purifying and allowing my body to hold an ever-increasing vibration.

Once you turn down this path, it won't necessarily be easy. Your life will change. Your perceptions will change. You are growing, and some of the things that once seemed difficult will appear downright easy, and yet some ordinary things may become extraordinarily challenging.

Use your awakening experiences and all of the attendant phenomena for your spiritual growth, but be careful not to identify too much with them or they will ultimately limit your spiritual growth. Always be open to more, to moving beyond what is before you at the moment. Your own spiritual evolution, the raising of your vibration, is much more important than any phenomena described here. But you can use those phenomena to assist in increasing your vibration.

You came here to learn, experience, evolve and serve, as only you can. Remember who you are.

I have much love for you on your journey.

Be well,

Wendy

Notes

Introduction

1 Hawkins, David, R., *I: Reality and Subjectivity* (West Sedona, Arizona: Veritas Publishing, 2003), p. 419.

2 Ibid, p. 419.

3 Tolle, Eckhart, *A New Earth: Awakening to Your Life's Purpose* (New York, New York: A Plume Book, Penguin Group, 2006), p. 309.

4 Ibid, p. 17.

5 Ibid, p. 259.

6 Ibid, p. 19.

7 Virtue, Doreen and Brown, Lynnette, *Angel Numbers: The angels explain the meaning of 111, 444 and other numbers in your life* (Carlsbad, California: Hay House, Inc., 2005), p. 86.

Chapter 1

Energy: Can You Feel It?

1 Virtue, Doreen, *Angels and Ascended Masters: A guide to working and healing with divinities and deities* (Carlsbad, California: Hay House, Inc., 2003).

Chapter 3

Allowing and Prayer: Be Open

1 The Holy Bible, Psalms 46:10 (King James Version)

2 Hawkins, David R., *Power Vs. Force: The hidden determinants of human behavior* (Carlsbad, California: Hay House, Inc., 2002), p. 295.

3 Emoto, Masaru, *The Hidden Messages in Water* (New York, New York: Atria Books, 2004).

4 The Holy Bible, John 16:24 (American Standard Version)

5 Blackburn Losey, Meg, on World Puja Network, *Power of Life* show hosted by Maureen Moss, April 27, 2006, www.worldpuja.com archives.

Chapter 5
Awakenings: Everybody Up!

1 Virtue, Doreen and Brown, Lynnette, *Angel Numbers: The angels explain the meaning of 111, 444 and other numbers in your life* (Carlsbad, California: Hay House, Inc., 2005), p. 24.

2 Ibid, p. 26

Chapter 7
Fluctuations: Here We Go Again

1 The Holy Bible, Matthew 9:20-22 (Revised Standard Version).

Chapter 10
Know Your Power: You Are Powerful

1 The Holy Bible, John 14:12. (Revised Standard Version)

2 Ilibagiza, Immaculee, *Left to Tell: Discovering God amidst the Rwandan holocaust* (Carlsbad, California: Hay House, Inc., 2006).

3 Hawkins, David, R., *Power Vs. Force: The hidden determinants of human behavior* (Carlsbad, California: Hay House, Inc., 2002), p. 132.

Chapter 14
Jesus: Just a Regular Guy

1 *A Course in Miracles* (California: Foundation for Inner Peace, 1996).

2 The Holy Bible, John 14:12. (Revised Standard Version)

3 The Holy Bible, Matthew 10:8 (Revised Standard Version)

4 The Holy Bible, Matthew 10:40 (King James Version)

5   The Holy Bible, Matthew 10:24-25 (King James Version)

6   Chopra, Deepak, *The Third Jesus: The Christ We Cannot Ignore* (New York: Harmony Books, 2008).

7   Hawkins, David, R., *Power Vs. Force: The hidden determinants of human behavior* (Carlsbad, California: Hay House, Inc., 2002), p.68.

Chapter 15
Ghosts: Who's There?

1   Cunningham, Lowell and Solomon, Ed, *Men in Black,* Amblin Entertainment, 1997.

2   Ibid

About the Author

Wendy Joy worked for eighteen years as a Speech Language Pathologist in a prestigious brain trauma center. She left that work to pursue writing and practice alternative healing techniques. She is a Reiki Master Teacher and is also certified in Integrated Energy Therapy,® Past Life Regression, Dysfunctional Core Belief Release, Crystal Layout Therapy, Essential Oil Treatment, Chakra Balancing, Vibrational Alignment, Underlying Cause Identification, Release of Earthbound Spirits, Emotional Release and Spiritual Journeys. She received her bachelors degrees in Psychology and English from Duke University and her masters degree in Speech Language Pathology from Rutgers University. A native of New Jersey, Wendy now resides on the North Carolina coast with her husband and two children. She regularly speaks on topics related to healing and the spiritual awakening process.

To contact Wendy Joy or learn more, visit www.wendyjoy.net.

Like Wendy Joy on Facebook and participate in free monthly energy work for all those on the page.

A portion of the author's royalties from this book are being donated to charity.

www.ingramcontent.com/pod-product-compliance
Lightning Source LLC
Chambersburg PA
CBHW022018090426
42739CB00006BA/185